# Staying Sober

# Staying Sober

*Tips for Working a Twelve Step
Program of Recovery*

M EREDITH  G OULD

50th
1949-1999
HAZELDEN

HAZELDEN®

INFORMATION & EDUCATIONAL SERVICES

Hazelden
Center City, Minnesota 55012-0176

1-800-328-0094
1-651-213-4590 (Fax)
www.hazelden.org

Library of Congress Cataloging-in-Publication Data

Gould, Meredith, 1951–
    Staying sober : tips for working a twelve step program of recovery
/ Meredith Gould.
        p.    cm.
    ISBN 1-56838-340-1
    1. Alcoholics—Rehabilitation.    2. Alcoholics—Rehabilitation Case
studies.    3. Twelve-step programs.    4. Alcoholics Anonymous.
I.Title.
HV5278.G68    1999
362.292'86—dc21                                                          99-32564
                                                                              CIP


03 02 01 00 99    6 5 4 3 2 1

Author's Note
The Twelve Steps and other AA materials, excerpted from *Alcoholics Anonymous,* are reprinted with the permission of Alcoholics Anonymous World Services, Inc. Permission to reprint and adapt the Twelve Steps, and to reprint the additional AA material, does not mean that AA has reviewed or approved the contents of this publication, nor that AA necessarily agrees with the views expressed herein. AA is a program of recovery from alcoholism *only*—use of AA material in connection with non-AA publications, or in any other non-AA context, does not imply otherwise.

Opinions embedded within this text are solely those of the author. Anyone feeling perturbed, disturbed, or outraged is encouraged to "turn it over."

Cover design by Madeline Berglund
Interior design by Donna Burch
Typesetting by Stanton Publication Services, Inc.

# Dedication

*For those who have the guts and grace to do the work of recovery.*

# Contents

# Preface

Was my "story" the most irrelevant, unrelatable one on Planet Recovery or what? I certainly thought it was, until the night I told it at an inpatient rehab.

Despite my abiding belief in the power of service, I had gone to that speaking commitment profoundly unthrilled—and slightly miffed—that my sponsor dared suggest such a thing. Jeepers, what did I have to say to these women? I hadn't gone through a rehab. Hadn't needed to because I wasn't all that visibly messed up. (The poop hit the proverbial fan of life *after* I decided to sober up, an experience I would discover was by no means unique to me.)

While family and friends certainly thought I had a few "issues," no one had pegged me as Twelve Step program material. After all, everything I did to excess was either purely situational, secretive, or bush league when compared to the addictive predilections of intimate partners.

I got my butt into a Twelve Step program after I had not one, but two so-called moments of clarity. First, I actually saw myself doing something only a (fill in the blank) would do. A few weeks later, I actually caught myself thinking something only a (fill in the blank) would think. At last, I had hit what one friend calls "Step Zero" (i.e., This s**t has got to stop). I needed, but more important, wanted, my life to be different.

While I thought these revelations might be moderately interesting, they were hardly dramatic enough to serve as a cautionary tale. Oh, my boring little suburban story. No need to mention driving on hallucinogens because I did that back in the early 1970s with my sorority sisters. No street drugs, just routine stockpiling of postsurgical prescriptions. Okay, so occasionally I'd "borrow" meds from other people's medicine cabinets. I had never been fired. Whatever stern lectures I ever got about my attitude may or may not have been linked to off-hour activities. No arrests. No party puking. No Repo Man ever showed up for stuff I acquired during shopping binges. No one ever had to rush me to a hospital for a good stomach pumping. Okay, so maybe the vanilla extract episode was worth mentioning. Mostly, I engaged in a lot screaming and sobbing. Occasionally, I would hurl small appliances. These were behavioral glitches that I blamed on hormones whenever possible.

So, off I went to this rehab and rambled through my ho-hum-who-cares story, one that I would eventually realize illustrates the inexorable and progressive nature of addiction. Afterwards, a woman who looked and sounded absolutely nothing like me thanked me profusely for telling her story. Huh?

I felt my mind blink a few times as I slowly connected the dots: If *she* was in a rehab and we had the same story, then I could've been in a rehab too. So I *was* Twelve Step program material. It was one of those yippee/darn moments that I've come to cherish in recovery.

Which Twelve Step program am I in? None of your beeswax (although I am just fine with revealing in print that I am totally powerless over cats). Let's just say that without straining my brain I could easily come up with about seven that would have me.

Despite an abundance of Twelve Step program choices, I opted to initially—and for a change—dive fully into *just one*. Doing so has worked well for me. I am not the person I was before I started "working the program," and that's a good thing! Like everyone else who truly opts for recovery, I had no idea how different everything would eventually get. Today, I am someone who is not at all adverse to prefacing my in-the-rooms "sharing" with all that goopy Twelve Step lingo about gratitude for "the grace of God, these Steps, and the fellowship."

Now, about my reasons for writing this book.

First, I am an unapologetically huge fan of Twelve Step recovery. Step work does not represent my first foray into the wild world of personal growth and healing. But of all the workshops, training sessions, one-on-one therapy sessions, and guided study courses in which I have participated, I can easily say that Step work has been one of—if not the—most durable life-changing activities I've experienced.

I like the simplicity, emphasis on self-responsibility, and spiritual focus of recovery programs that are based on the Twelve Steps of Alcoholics Anonymous. I have seen the Steps and other program activities work in my life and in the lives of others.

Of course, being the well-trained social scientist that I am, I know darn well that no one has scientifically proven that Twelve Step programs work. And I know there are recovery programs around that are purportedly less sexist, more secular, less structured, and more permissive. At the same time, I know that Twelve Step programs are exactly what doctors, psychotherapists, social workers, and clergy invariably recommend after everything else has failed. I believe these professional helpers do so because they understand and respect the enormous healing power of receiving daily unconditional support. I believe they do so because even the most rabid atheists among them recognize that addiction is a phenomenon whose source is bigger, deeper, and a much more subtle matter than wacky brain biochemistry or incompetent parents.

Another thing: When I first started my own Twelve Step recovery, I read everything I possibly could and understood almost none of it. It didn't matter that I was overeducated, a writer myself, and an avid reader. Suddenly, the words were too big, the paragraphs too long, and the typeface too small. It was mostly an attention-span thing. I simply could not concentrate long enough to comprehend what I was reading.

Then, as the fog started to lift a bit, I got my undies in a wad over the way "official literature" was written. I thought it was too archaic, too sentimental, and too dense. Eventually, I stopped with the literary critique and channeled my energy into listening. Still, that didn't stop me from wanting to make my own contribution to the recovery literature. If anything, lots of thought-provoking listening got me thinking about actually moving into action. (Twelve Step programs tend to spark that trajectory!) What you're reading is the end result of that process.

This book is organized around the key principles that underlie all Twelve Step programs of recovery. It doesn't really matter which specific addiction—alcohol, drugs, gambling, nicotine, overeating, sex, or shopping—is wrecking your life. If you want to quit and pursue recovery through a Twelve Step program, you'll need to stop using, attend meetings, reach out to others, "work" the Twelve Steps, and help others stay clean, sober, and abstinent. Each of these aspects, therefore, rates its own chapter of short practical tips. You do not necessarily have to read these chapters in sequence and certainly not in one sitting—unless you've already been to a meeting, called your sponsor, done some Step work, reached out to help another still-suffering whatever, and have the time at your disposal today!

As you read, you may begin to notice that some statements look suspiciously like my *opinions*. Bingo! They are. Rest assured, nothing in this book is meant to represent the last—or any—official word on anything having to do with Twelve Step recovery. As we say around the rooms, "Take what you want and leave the rest."

Hey, if your experience is anything like mine, you'll find that recovery is a terrific, annoying, fabulous, horrible, illuminating, confusing lifelong adventure. I hope this book will serve to help guide your journey—one amazing day at a time.

# Acknowledgments

Oh, where to begin? By thanking God, of course, for recovery, cats, friends, and all around joie de vivre.

Writing this particular book at this particular time in my life has been quite the adventure. I simply could not have done it without the creative, emotional, spiritual, and gastronomic support of wonderful friends. To properly list everyone would make me more nuts than I already am. Nevertheless, I must name some key players in the game of creative life.

Huge thanks to Katherine Boyle of Veritas agency. I doubt there's a brighter, more encouraging, and more diligent agent out there. Thank you, Steve Lehman of Hazelden for inciting me to write in my own voice. Thanks, Mommy (aka, Gerry Gould) for the pep notes. Thanks, of course, to Regina Catalano and Suzin Green, key members of my creative brain trust for this project. Special thanks to Rick Gregg who graciously allows for living amends.

And now . . . the recovery community.

I've heard tell about the extreme affection and loyalty people in recovery feel toward those who were there for them since day—and Step—one. I'm no exception and would especially like to thank all the characters who attend the 7:15 A.M., Monday Step Study and Promises meetings at the 24 Club. Please buy my book so I can afford to put more than one buck in the basket.

I do, however, want to get somewhat less anonymous about two program people. First, the wise and wonderful Jim Q., of blessed memory. He plunked me down, listened in that gently incisive way he had, asked questions, then encouraged me to go ahead with this book. Second, I must mention my spectacular sponsor. By divine providence, I have a sponsor who is not only compassionate, gentle, and extremely well-grounded in Twelve Step recovery but also literate and editorially savvy. She read this entire manuscript and laughed in all the right places. Thank you, Paula W.

# Introduction

In the beginning, there was Bill Wilson.

Well, not exactly. In the very beginning, there were drunks in gutters, Bowery bums, and the family disgrace who was guaranteed to make a scene at weddings, bar mitzvahs, graduations, and wakes.

And so, there were biblical injunctions. For a while, there was Prohibition. There were mental hospitals for the hopeless cases and, ultimately, quiet graves.

In 1935, a failed stockbroker named Bill Wilson managed to abstain from drinking for one more day by spilling his guts about wanting to drink to Dr. Bob Smith.

It's not as if Bill W. hadn't made any earlier attempts to sober up. By the time he was thirty-six (1931), his drinking was out of control and way beyond being influenced by the tears and pleas of his faithful wife, Lois. According to history—and probably some legend—several experiences led up to Bill's epiphany in 1935. By 1934, he had heard about how the Oxford Group, an unabashedly Christian home-based prayer meeting, had some minor success with thoroughbred alcoholics. He attended some of their meetings, but that didn't stop him from ending up drunk and in a hospital once again. There, after crying out for help, he had a hugely spectacular "white light" experience (which some speculate may be chalked up to withdrawal hallucinations fueled by belladonna, the treatment of choice at the time). This, he believed, represented not only his ultimate release from drinking, but the Divine revelation that helping others would help him stay sober. Well, six months of proselytizing didn't exactly work as he had anticipated. By May 1935, Bill stood in a hotel lobby in Akron, Ohio, totally bummed after another lousy business deal, deciding whether or not to get loaded.

Well, he didn't. Instead, he found his way to Dr. Bob and yakked his ear off about drinking for over six hours. Misery, it turned out, really did love company. After that, not only was Bill W. done with drinking but so, in time, was Dr. Bob. These two eventually started the mother of all Twelve Step programs, Alcoholics Anonymous.

This is not the place to go into the entire history of Alcoholics Anonymous, the infamous sauerkraut and cold-tomato cure, or the early internecine battles that gave rise to the Twelve Steps and Twelve Traditions. Suffice it to say that since all this happened over sixty years ago, nearly two million people in 141 countries attend AA meetings. Additional Twelve Step programs have sprouted like, well, sprouts.

Back in 1994, popular news magazines were reporting that in the United States alone over fifteen million people attend at least one (if not more) of the 500,000 self-help groups. The vast majority of these groups are based on the Twelve Steps of Alcoholics Anonymous. A few, such as Al-Anon (founded, 1953), Narcotics Anonymous (founded, 1953), and Overeaters Anonymous (founded, 1960), emerged as Alcoholics Anonymous gained credibility during the first few decades of its existence. The rest seem to have bloomed into being as the personal growth movement took off during the 1970s and 1980s, their emergence being more organic than strategic.

There's no shortage of Twelve Step programs. Check out this short list: Adult Children of Alcoholics, ARTS (Artists Recovering through the Twelve Steps), Cocaine Anonymous, Codependents Anonymous, Debters Anonymous, Dual Disorders Anonymous, Emotions Anonymous, Gamblers Anonymous,

Incest Survivors Anonymous, Nicotine Anonymous, Pill Anonymous, Sex Addicts Anonymous, Sexual Compulsives Anonymous, Sex and Love Addicts Anonymous, Shoplifters Anonymous, Spenders Anonymous, and Workaholics Anonymous. There's even a Twelve Step program for those who are a little too pathologically stuck on recovery—Recoveries Anonymous!

There's also no shortage of "alternative" recovery programs, emerging primarily in reaction to the alleged authoritarianism, sexism, narcissism, and overt spiritual emphasis of traditional Twelve Step programs: Rational Recovery, Moderation Management, Secular Organizations for Sobriety, Sixteen Steps, and SMART (Self-Management and Recovery Training). Still, these well-established challengers share with traditional Twelve Step programs a belief in the power of group support.

Love 'em or disdain 'em, the impact of Twelve Step programs is undeniable. Today, the "slogans" (e.g., "One day at a time") are a familiar feature of contemporary Western culture. Program-based idioms (e.g., "What's your story?"), no matter how sardonically invoked, are embedded in colloquial English. The notion that one must "hit bottom" before actually doing anything about addiction and the suggestion that addiction is indeed a disease of body, mind, and spirit comes from the work and insights of AA's founders. This, if you choose to traipse the well-trodden path to recovery, is your legacy. Personally, I think it's all kind of cool when I stop to think about it.

# 1
## Don't Use

"Don't use!" Sure seems like a no brainer, doesn't it? Of course your *chances of staying stopped* will increase enormously if you don't pick up an addictive substance or activity in the first place. And yet this simple, fundamental advice can be excruciatingly difficult to follow.

First off, virtually nothing is ever intuitively obvious to an addict. If it were, many, if not most, addictions would cease to exist. What sane person would willingly use a substance that kills brain cells, scrambles the central nervous system, wipes out organ systems, destroys relationships, and ultimately leads to either incarceration or death?

But, for most people, logic has little to do with the addictive process, because the very nature of addiction is such that if the substance or activity doesn't have a lock on the body, it most assuredly has one on the psyche. Some addictions, like those involving alcohol, drugs, nicotine, caffeine, and sugar, are indisputably linked to physiology. Others, like a compulsive need to gamble, shop, work, and be in a relationship (including one with a rigidly formalistic religious community), involve what are seemingly more elusive psychological hungers. Then, of course, there are all sorts of hybrid addictions involving both body and mind, such as overeating, sex, and exercise.

These distinctions may blur or disappear altogether as an addiction progresses. Physiological cravings invariably evolve into psychological yearnings. Psychological compulsions more often than not manifest physiologically when thwarted. This, in turn, may lead the addict to replace an activity with a substance. Addictions, it seems, come in layers which are better peeled than ripped off.

It's pretty darned complex. It's also pretty darned simple. No matter what the origin or initial manifestation of addiction might be, it ain't gonna stop until you do. That means putting down the booze, drugs, or cigarettes; swearing off gambling or shopping; taking a long enough break from sex and relationships to sober up in that department; and learning how to use food, work, and exercise in moderation. Cleanup can be a daunting prospect, especially for anyone who has multiple addictions (and there are precious few who don't). That, by the way, is why Twelve Step programs recommend doing this work "One day at a time."

Let the tips in this chapter help you tackle this important preliminary step. After all, while getting sober may be tough, it's a lot easier to stay sober once you're already there; so, "Don't use."

## CHAPTER TIPS

☞ Even before your head totally clears, make an effort to learn what addiction does to your body as well as your mind. Read everything you can, attend public lectures, and watch television specials. Becoming an expert on the physiological consequences of your particular addiction not only will help you treat addiction like the progressive disease it is, but will also equip you to eventually help others. In addition, understanding the physical factors may clarify why you

- can't handle "just one" drink, fix, puff, taste, or pill
- feel depressed or anxious even when things appear to be going well

- have certain persistent health problems
- may develop particular health problems in the future
- can't remember diddly-squat

☞ While you're at it, study up on the behavioral traits of addicts and what the recovery process involves. If you went through a formal rehabilitation program at a treatment center, you were probably exposed to much of this information. Still, chances are you remain a little fuzzy on the details. If you never learned this stuff to begin with, you owe it to yourself to learn it now. Knowing more about the addictive personality not only will provide insight into your own machinations, but will also help you understand others around you, like your new best friends in recovery.

> **"If you don't do anything to make it better, it will get worse."**

☞ Since addicts are generally impatient and quick-fix oriented, you want to *make it massively inconvenient* to use your substance of choice. This is no guarantee of recovery, but it can't hurt, for example, to

- keep alcohol, binge foods, cigarettes, drugs, or pornography out of your home.
- dump the snazzy barware, wine glasses, beer mugs, and brandy snifters into recycling or donate them for a rummage sale.
- remove suggestive items such as powdered sugar or baking soda (which look like cocaine); sage (an "energy clearing" herb that smells like dope); flavoring extracts (containing a remarkable amount of alcohol); and evocative paraphernalia like handheld mirrors, ashtrays, the object d'art that looks like a bong, and the music or incense you used to create a mood or cover up your using.

- destroy all credit cards and use cash only. Don't even think about getting an ATM card and forget debit cards as well.
- make your home, car, and workplace off-limits for smoking and drinking.
- contact your cable company about blocking out the shopping networks if you can't resist watching them. Better yet, cancel your cable service or get rid of the television altogether, because zoned-out compulsive TV watching seems to cut across all addictions.
- take your name off consumer catalog lists by sending all versions of your name and address to: Mail Preference Service, c/o Direct Marketing Association, Box 9008, Farmingdale, New York 11735-9008.
- dial the phone and talk to another addict *before* using or picking up.

☛ Map out new driving or walking routes so that you go nowhere near "your" neighborhood bar, the liquor stores, the corner where you used to cop, or the park where you used.

☛ *Clean up your addictions in life-threatening order.* Tackling everything at once is a surefire recipe for disaster. If you drink alcoholically and smoke cigarettes, it probably makes sense to sober up before quitting nicotine, which is physiologically more addictive. If you use cocaine and gamble, you're probably wise to handle your drug addiction first. Unsure of what order in which to proceed? Ask yourself the following questions: What will kill me quickly? What will kill me slowly? What will destroy my brain? What will land me in jail?

☛ If you're visually oriented, creating a chart depicting the history of your addiction will help you literally see the progression of your substance use and abuse. Draw a time line that notes when you first started using and what you started with; then use graphics (e.g., boxes, circles, arrows) to show how your addictions have morphed and multiplied over time. You may, for example, have started out with inhalants, began smoking cigarettes, added alcohol, then switched to drugs for a while before returning to alcohol, then quit smoking and quit drinking but picked up compulsive eating and working like a lunatic before going back to whatever finally got you to try a Twelve Step fellowship.

☞ It may seem too simple to be true, but one way to stay stopped or quit is to not start. Even one drink, cigarette, pill, lottery ticket, peep show, on-sale item, bite, or whatever can snare you in the web of addiction. Besides setting a physiological response in motion, the first one of anything leads to the psychological illusion of control which usually manifests in such famous last words as "I can stop at any time," "Just this once," "After this one, I'll never do it again," and the ever popular "See, nothing bad happened."

> "You never know what you're addicted to until you stop."

*So, how not to start?* First, use experience to think through what will happen after the initial glow. Don't cheat! Follow this story through to the very end, which may include puking your guts out, being totally broke, or waking up somewhere mighty strange. Either say this out loud or write it out.

If you can't talk yourself out of picking up again this way, *decide to start up your addiction again tomorrow.* It truly is amazing what a difference a day makes, especially if you spend the next twenty-four hours talking to other Twelve Steppers, praying for relief, and doing some rigorous First Step work. Then again, all you might need is a good meal and more sleep.

☞ Twelve Step lore has it that an addict can't be scared into quitting. Nevertheless, this simple arithmetic exercise might make you think twice about starting up again.

On a sheet of paper, calculate how much money you spent on your addiction during your last year of using. Include how much you spent on the substance itself, the cost of your time involved in using, and how much you had to dole out in gifts to smooth things over with infuriated family members, friends, or co-workers. Add in whatever you shelled out for bail, insurance surcharges, and attorney fees.

If you're in recovery for sex addiction, you'll need to tally the bucks you spent on alcohol and/or other drugs to numb your shame in addition to all the moolah you blew on porno magazines and videos, at peep shows, and for prostitutes. Don't forget whatever you spent on medical treatment for syphilis, gonorrhea, chlamydia, pelvic inflammatory disease, or (God forbid) that really big ticket disease, AIDS.

Scared yet?

☞ Feeling a mongo-huge shop-a-thon coming on? Make a written list of everything you think you absolutely must have or simply want. Don't buy a thing and review the list after thirty days. If you can remember what was so darned spectacular about the item, then maybe you can buy it—with cash. Even better: Put it on the list for another thirty days and see if you still want or need yet another set of drill bits, cookware, piece of jewelry, or pair of shoes.

☞ Use a body-scan technique to discover how you're really feeling. Closing your eyes to maximize concentration, mentally scan your body from head to toe. Notice how your shoulders, arms, and hands feel. Sweep your awareness down your front and up your back, from the outside of your body to the inside beat of your heart and movement of your breath. You can do this standing up or sitting down. Once you master this technique, you can scan your whole body in seconds.

The early warning signals of feeling addictive urges may masquerade as excitement, arousal, or anxiety. What you need to know is that heart palpitations, shortness of breath, a rush of adrenaline, tingling sensations, and a quickening of your pulse are all warning signals worth noticing. Since these physiological reactions always precede mental rationalizations, you can short-circuit the predictable mental gymnastics by focusing on what your body feels like. Using a body scan both heightens your awareness about what's going on and gives you enough time to let your rational mind take over.

☞ Ah, workplace holiday gifts from grateful vendors and salespeople! Don't let the loot leave the office with you. Give that magnificent bottle of brandy, big box of chocolate truffles, and the fruit 'n' cheese basket the size of Rhode Island to co-workers.

## Whoa, Trigger . . . H.A.L.T!

You can do yourself a huge favor by using H.A.L.T., a handy mnemonic device to trace your unwanted addictive feelings to being either Hungry, Angry, Lonely, or Tired. There are few, if any, addicts on the face of the earth whose addiction isn't massively triggered by one of these factors. You're headed for even deeper trouble if all apply and aren't quickly addressed. Fortunately, it's pretty easy to take care of yourself once you figure out what's knocked you off balance.

Hungry? Well, when was the last time you ate? And what did you eat? Oh really? You may need only a high protein or complex carbohydrate snack to get back on course. Or you may need a complete meal. In any case, a cookie and cup of java isn't sufficient.

Angry? Okay, what or who pissed you off this time? Is this something you can actually do anything about, or is it just life happening? When did you last get some aerobic exercise? Take a deep breath, take a nice hot bath, or write hate mail you never send. Let it go for now because nothing ever gets properly resolved out of anger. And if you believe this might be something worth getting wasted over, make a bunch of phone calls to other Twelve Steppers and ask them if they agree.

Lonely? Hmmm, are you feeling "lonely" or are you just not used to be alone? Did you get to a meeting today? Did you call your sponsor? Do you *have* a sponsor yet? Pick up that two-hundred-million-pound phone, call another Twelve Stepper to say, "I'm feeling lonely," then watch what happens.

Tired? Be honest, what kind of schedule are you keeping? Are you working extra hours? Are you futzing around until the wee hours when you should be in bed? Are you still plagued by everyone's recovery bugaboo—insomnia? You may need a nice hot bath, soothing music, a short snooze during a meeting, or, if you can swing it, a midday nap. At the very least, start going to sleep and waking up on a regular schedule.

## Got Food Issues?

So everyone keeps mentioning this H.A.L.T thing, but you also have "food issues," which means that recommendations to eat are cruel and unusual. Right? Wrong.

Because eating, unlike booze, cigarettes, smack, or shopping, is indeed essential for life, recovery for food addicts—cross-addicted or not—is complex. At the beginning of their recovery, addicts who struggle with obesity because of overeating sometimes mistakenly think that food is the culprit. Paradoxically, so do those who look skeletal because they struggle with anorexia nervosa.

This is not the place to go fully into it, but both over- and undereating are usually about hungers other than physiological. At the same time, years of goofy, dangerous diets have depleted the body of important nutrients and wrecked the metabolism, so hunger may indeed be physiologically based. Add to that the fact that thirst and exhaustion may also masquerade as hunger, and the "hungry, angry, lonely, and tired" checklist seems irrelevant.

Still, chances are that many, if not all, the same conditions that drive other addicts to use are driving you to abuse food. You will need to ask when, what, why, and how much you last ate whenever you feel hungry. You will have to be careful about compulsively exercising to diffuse anger. You, too, need to call others in recovery and head for bed instead of the refrigerator when you're feeling tired.

For tips about keeping a food diary, choosing a nutritionally balanced food plan, and cooking healthy, take a field trip to the health section of your local bookstore or holistic health emporium. Try to avoid the trendy diet du jour books and look for guides that have been in print forever (e.g., *Food and Healing* by Annemarie Colbin, Ballantine, 1986). You'll also want to avoid being seduced by the slick fitness magazines racked, interestingly, right by the gum, candy, and tabloids at your local supermarket. More often than not, they're the primary source of the latest fad diet plans they recycle over and over. Just when you've settled into grapefruit, they switch to celery leaves with cayenne pepper and boiled potato eyes. Stick with the classics.

☞ Manage the urge to use by

- reciting Step One: "We admitted we were powerless over [you know what]—that our lives had become unmanageable."
- reading up on Step One in a Step book and attending as many First Step meetings as you can find.
- writing a Step One autobiography in which you give examples of your powerlessness, your attempts to control, and how you increasingly lost control over time. To develop a more accurate understanding of "unmanageability," *describe in lurid detail* the impact your addiction had on your public and private lives. Don't forget to include the weird, dangerous, or nutso stuff you did while under the influence.

☞ If writing isn't your thing, visuals can be potent reminders. Flip through magazines, collect images that represent the effects of your addiction, and paste them up into a collage. Or collect them in a folder that you look through when you think you've had just about enough recovery. Remember to include photos of yourself at the height (or depth) of your addiction.

> "You have to be willing to participate in your own recovery."

☞ As you sober up, you will probably feel moved at some point to take better care of your external environment. Don't be surprised if—as you go through closets, drawers, or your car's trunk—you come across abandoned evidence of your addiction. This may take the form of a long-forgotten pill stash, old joints, a box of half-eaten chocolates, or a few bottles not yet fully drained. Your best bet is to immediately call someone else in the program to tell on yourself as you toss this stuff out. If you're very early in recovery or feeling particularly vulnerable, ask someone to come over to physically help you get rid of this junk.

☞ Traveling? Do the following, especially during early recovery:
- Stay away from cruise ships, which are really floating bars, casinos, and endless buffets. You wanna cruise the seas, but not high? Ask your travel agent or check the Internet for information about cruise lines offering "clean and sober" vacations.
- Either travel with someone who doesn't get distracted by airport bars and in-flight drinks or organize yourself so you don't have time to sniff around. If you're strapped in next to someone who is buying up the entire liquor cart, ask the flight attendant to let you switch seats.
- At hotels, refuse a key to the in-room snack and liquor bar. If you think you might try to beat it open with your complimentary copy of the morning newspaper, ask that the bad goodies be removed before you settle in.

☞ Be sure to tell (or remind) doctors and dentists that you're in recovery *before* they start prescribing medications for pain, inflammation, depression, or anxiety. Make your recovery status known before scheduling any surgical procedure. Addicts and alcoholics in particular seem to be more metabolically sensitive to certain drugs and are generally at greater risk for drug interactions. The "standard" dosage for a non-addict may be totally wrong for you. Honestly and directly revealing that you're in recovery could literally save your life.

☞ If you absolutely must take a narcotic medication for pain, ask the doctor to write a prescription that directs the pharmacist to dispense only a few pills at a time. You can also ask someone immune to the seductive charms of drugs to hold the medication for you and to make sure you take one pill every four hours instead of four pills every hour.

☞ Take treatment and medication suggestions from well-meaning Twelve Steppers only if they happen to also be bona fide medical practitioners. There is no shortage of doctors, dentists, and nurses in Twelve Step programs, some of whom will generously dispense free advice. Go ahead and troll for other opinions; but, in the end, check with someone who is qualified to understand your particular case.

The only possible exception to this has to do with advice on the use of vitamins, minerals, and herbs. The average holistic health enthusiast generally knows more than most traditionally trained doctors about complementary medicine.

☞ Explore holistic health options for dealing with medical problems that emerge in recovery. As a general rule, holistic health practitioners are better able to treat the whole person—body, mind, and spirit—than are traditionally trained doctors, are committed to educating patients about self-care, and more frequently offer non-addictive strategies for pain management and treatment.

Look for a holistic health practitioner who is knowledgeable about addictions and willing to work in conjunction with conventional doctors. (Alas, you may be a bit challenged to find a doctor who is equally willing to work in conjunction with a holistic health practitioner.)

Modalities to check out include nutrition therapy, acupuncture, homeopathy, and Ayurveda. Where to begin? Look in the phone book; then conduct brief phone interviews for an initial vibe. Don't forget to ask around after Twelve Step meetings for referrals, keeping in mind that you're soliciting opinions which are not necessarily "The Truth."

## Is There Any Point to Acupuncture?

Isn't it amazing how addicts who think nothing of sticking all sorts of substances into their bodies start wincing mightily at the mere mention of acupuncture needles?

If you were being treated five thousand years ago, you'd have good reason to cringe. Then, practitioners pressed pointed stones against meridian points to relieve certain physiological conditions. Pointed stones eventually gave way to iron needles, until the modern technique of inserting fine, steel needles at those points developed.

Acupuncture needles, which are designed to push through skin without damaging tissue, nerve, or blood vessels, are as fine as hair, flexible, and have rounded tips. They are so unobtrusive that many patients relax into sleep during treatments.

According to Chinese medicine, organs are part of larger systems linked together by meridians, or energy pathways, throughout the body. Today, practitioners still use the 14 main meridians and 365 specific points discovered by the ancient Chinese.

Acupuncture is extremely effective in managing withdrawal, assisting detoxification, and reducing cravings for any number of addictive substances. Since the late 1980s, several scientific studies have shown that adding acupuncture to a treatment program for chronic alcoholics and those addicted to cocaine, crack, heroin, nicotine, and opiates significantly reduces their relapse rate. Auriculotherapy (ear acupuncture) has also been used to successfully treat sex, gambling, work, and food addictions.

Plus, acupuncture's amazing ability to reduce pain and induce relaxation by stimulating the body's natural release of endorphins and other hormones makes it a safe

alternative to medications that, even when properly prescribed, can hook addicts and alcoholics back into the
cycle of addiction. While it won't heal the psychological
or spiritual components of addiction, acupuncture is considered an extremely safe and effective way to tackle the
physiological aspects.

While you're at it, there's an entire world of body-mind
practices that can help you manage some of the physical and
emotional pain that inevitably emerges during recovery. These
include everything from simple Swedish-style massage to more
esoteric energy-based approaches such as polarity. Also available are Western contemporary movement-oriented modalities
such as the Alexander Technique and the Feldenkrais Method,
as well as Eastern movement arts like Hatha Yoga and Qi Quong.

Where to begin? Your local health club, day spa, and
YWCA/YMCA probably offer classes or private sessions in one
or more of these approaches. Your best bet is the word-of-mouth
recommendations of others in recovery, although ultimately
you'll have to decide whether a particular modality (or its practitioner) is for you.

Caution: Wait until you have at least a year of continuous recovery before dabbling in these very powerful modalities.

If you want to try yoga, study with a teacher who has
practiced and taught for several years. In addition to being qualified to teach the postures of hatha yoga, the teacher should
know how to guide you through the various yogic breathing
techniques.

Although it is often touted as an excellent form of exercise,
yoga also has a powerful impact on body, mind, and spirit.
Under the guidance of a competent teacher, yoga can be extremely healing for people in recovery. It is known to release

deeply held body-based trauma, which means it can trigger a fairly deep level of catharsis. Confidentially revealing to your teacher that you're in recovery will explain why, while everyone else is happily hanging out in the "Fish," you have burst into uncontrollable sobs.

☞ Begin to get into shape with simple, moderate exercise. Your body has probably been woefully neglected for quite a while (either that, or you've exercised like a lunatic and have any number of injuries) and will need all the tender loving care you can provide.

> "Move a muscle, change a mood!"

Start with a ten- to fifteen-minute walk every day, doing errands on foot, or taking stairs instead of elevators before signing up for weight training and a hip-hop class at the local fitness center.

## Breathe Your Way to Recovery

Long before recovery programs were invented, there were yogis who not only understood the powerful connection between body and mind, but made it into a science. Yoga is perhaps the oldest system of personal growth in existence. In fact, not much has changed over the past six thousand years, even though the classes you take today will be held in a gym, health club, or someone's living room rather than a temple. In addition to learning postures developed centuries ago to bring body, mind, and spirit into alignment, you'll learn something else—how to breathe.

Like most people, you breathe enough to stay alive, but not nearly enough to reduce stress or manage uncomfortable feelings. Healthy breathing is even more challenging if you're recovering from addiction because your body has gotten used to substituting substances for oxygen. As a result, you use an even smaller percentage of your available lung capacity. You may think you're breathing, but you're not.

Notice how you breathe as you read this. Does your breath seem to hover around your collarbone or throat? Do you feel like sighing? Right now, try taking a deep breath through your nostrils. Imagine filling your entire belly with air; then release your breath slowly and completely. Now, how do you feel? Calm? Dizzy? Focused? The breath is key to both relaxation and concentration, which is why it's such an important feature of yoga and the preparatory practice for meditation.

Yoga teaches that the breath is what connects body with mind. Control the breath, and the mind can be controlled as well—mind chatter can be stilled, negative self-talk silenced.

Physiologically, yogic breathing oxygenates the blood and gives your internal organs a great, natural massage. When you inhale fully, your abdomen expands and your diaphragm moves down to massage your abdominal organs. Exhale completely, and your heart gets massaged as your diaphragm moves up.

Yogic breathing is conscious and intentional, done through the nose with the exhale lasting at least twice as long as the inhale. Inhalation stimulates and exhalation relaxes. Start with learning the complete yogic breath which, because of its focus on the belly, abdomen, and chest, is also known as the "three-part breath." Here's how to do it:

• Lie on your back with your hands resting softly on your belly, fingertips touching. With your mouth closed, inhale fully. You'll know you've done this when your belly expands enough to separate your fingertips.

- Continue to inhale slowly, bringing the breath up through your abdomen, then up into your chest. Imagine that your lungs extend into your shoulders and fill your shoulders with breath.
- Now, with your mouth still closed, start to slowly exhale. Reversing the movement of breath, release it from your chest, abdomen, and belly. Squeeze out every last molecule of air.
- Repeat. Inhaling belly, abdomen, and chest. Exhaling chest, abdomen, and belly.

Try this basic yogic breath for five whole minutes. You'll probably feel an interesting—and possibly unfamiliar—combination of being relaxed and energized, calm and alert. With practice, you'll be able to use this breath while sitting, standing, or walking to reduce stress and relieve anxiety in many situations.

You've been chest breathing involuntarily nearly twenty-five thousand times a day since you were born. How will you ever remember to consciously breathe throughout your whole body? Frequent sighing is a sure sign of the "air hunger" resulting from shallow, irregular breathing. Take it as a sign that you need to focus more fully on your breath. Like sighing, yawning may indicate poor oxygenation, but it also relieves tension. *Yawns serve an important function, so try not to stifle yours.*

If you don't want to go the yoga route, you can do other things to get your breath moving fully and deeply. Sing in the shower, your car, or as you putter around your home. Watch a funny movie, hang out with a hilarious friend, or get to a meeting where you're bound to share some good laughs with others in recovery.

☞ Just because something is available at a health-food store does *not* mean it's healthy for you. Watch out for herbal remedies that come in alcohol tinctures. They may be as problematic for addicts as they are for alcoholics. Fortunately, the most frequently used remedies such as echinacea and goldenseal are available as alcohol-free liquids. You can also find them in capsule or tea form.

Read labels carefully when you shop for over-the-counter (OTC) medications for pain, inflammation, allergies, and other respiratory ailments. These preparations may include sedative-hypnotics, such as alcohol and codeine, or nervous system stimulants in the form of pseudoephedrine. There are safe, non-addictive herbal or homeopathic substitutes for all this stuff.

Still, because addicts are capable of getting psychologically hooked on substances that are supposedly not physiologically addictive, check your motives, or at least consider that you may be scamming yourself. Are you temporarily taking this herb to handle a bout of insomnia? Or are you secretly hoping for a space shot into the ozone?

## Is There Better Living through Chemistry?

One of the big debates in Twelve Step fellowships these days surrounds the use of what are generically called "antidepressants." With the growing popularity of drugs known as SSRIs (selective serotonin reuptake inhibitors), such as Prozac, Paxil, Zoloft, and medical evidence indicating that addicts and alcoholics may need to have serotonin levels more aggressively managed, this debate has recently reached epic and sometimes quite vituperative proportions.

On one side of the debate you have long-timers who claim that once the body detoxifies and the obsession to use has lifted, it's enough to work the Steps and call a sponsor. Emotional balance eventually comes with enough clean time and meeting attendance. These Twelve Steppers take a hard line against the use of any drug for depression, anxiety, or fear.

On the other side of the controversy are those who argue that depriving people in recovery of these particular medications is like taking insulin away from a diabetic. They will also point out how the SSRIs are not, strictly speaking, antidepressant, although they do have an antidepressant effect. These drugs were originally developed to break the cycles of obsessive-compulsive behaviors that frequently show up among addicts, especially those with eating disorders.

*Both sides are right!*

You can indeed achieve unprecedented levels of emotional stability and mental health by simply cleaning out your system, listening at meetings, and working the Twelve Steps. But, for some, this may simply not be enough. There's a difference between having the blues and being suicidally depressed, between feeling anxious and being paralyzed with terror, between being moody and having a multiple-personality disorder. Some mental and emotional imbalances are so overwhelming that they do require medical intervention in the form of medication that's much stronger than the serotonin reuptake inhibitors.

Beware of extremists at either end point of this debate. While veteran Twelve Steppers are (legitimately) big on diagnosing what is known as "terminal uniqueness," it is also true that brain biochemistry is somewhat like a fingerprint—yours will be different from theirs. The fact that you have time in recovery and faithfully attend meetings is eclipsed by screwy biochemistry.

If you have some clean time, are working the Steps and taking suggestions, but are still desperately miserable, you may need prescribed medication. But, be cautious. Unless your general practitioner is well-versed in both psychopharmacology and addiction, you could end up feeling worse. If you rely on a general practioner for mental health as well as physical health treatment, shop for one who knows about addictions, understands drug interactions, and respects the power of Twelve Step programs.

> "'No' is a complete sentence."

☞ Plan ways to take care of yourself if you absolutely must attend a social or family function that might put you at risk:

- Bring a Twelve Step friend along to keep you company.
- Use separate transportation so you can leave easily and early if you feel the need to bolt.
- Go late (after the cocktail hour) and leave early (before everyone gets whacked out).
- Scout out a telephone and excuse yourself to call someone on your phone list if things get too weird.

☞ If you're a recovering alcoholic and you're faced with an open bar, pay attention. You want to make sure the club soda, ginger ale, or tonic water you've ordered comes without any alcoholic flavoring. Hey, just wait one darned second: What *are* you doing in that situation to begin with? Have you discussed the advisability of this soiree with your sponsor? Do you have check-in and bail-out plans in place if it gets too intense for you?

If you simply *must* attend this gig, get a friend to make sure you get the club soda, sparkling water, plain tonic water, or juice you requested. Pick someone who doesn't think it would be cute or fun to spike your seltzer—preferably someone in the program.

☞ If just saying "no" seems too abrupt or awkward, develop other ways to get people off your case about partaking or participating in addictive substances or activities. Here are some suggestions in order of elaboration and humor:

> **"If you don't want to slip, stay out of slippery places."**

- No, thank you.
- Not right now.
- I'm allergic.
- I'm on a diet.
- My health is already shot.
- I'm done contributing to the national debt.
- I'm not a pretty sight once I get started.
- I gave it up for Lent. (This is particularly amusing if you're Buddhist, Jewish, or Muslim.)
- I've decided I don't like jail.
- No, thanks. I'm expected back at work on Monday.

☞ Use the slogan "One day at a time" to stay focused. You can murmur it to yourself like a mantra or write it over and over again like an elementary school handwriting exercise. You can even make it the object of meditation, contemplating the images and meanings that emerge when you reflect wholeheartedly on the phrase "One day at a time."

☞ If the concept of an entire day seems overwhelming, use smaller increments—one hour at a time, one minute at a time, one moment at a time—to stay anchored in the present.

☞ Generate a list of healthy distractions and use these to help manage addictive urges. Have exercise head the list. In addition to satisfying physical cravings by activating the brain's mesolimbic dopamine system, it is almost impossible to smoke, drink, eat, shop, gamble, shoot up, or what have you while lifting weights, taking a step-aerobic class, running, swimming, bike riding, or playing racquet sports. Other less strenuous activities on your list can include

- cleaning up or puttering around your home
- gardening, yard work, or repotting plants
- washing and waxing your car
- painting and other decorating projects
- pursuing a hobby that requires a significant level of concentration (e.g., model building, crossword puzzles) or one involving meditative and potentially relaxing repetition (e.g., needle crafts, furniture refinishing)
- bathing the dog—if you *really* need distraction, try bathing the cat
- singing or playing an instrument—consider joining a community orchestra or chorus
- doing volunteer work with a physical component (e.g., joining Habitat for Humanity, walking dogs for the local animal shelter, cooking and serving at a soup kitchen, doing Twelve Step work at the county detox center)
- reading, especially magazines you can't afford to buy, at the public library

Hint: Create this list in advance so you don't have to concoct options on the spot.

☞ *Get into the habit of substituting safe forms of self-soothing* for ones that eventually lead to death, insanity, or incarceration. Write these self-care activities out on little strips of paper and collect them in a jar; pull one out the next time you're feeling deprived and do it.

Here are some suggestions guaranteed to lift the spirit regardless of age, race, ethnicity, sex, or sexual orientation:

- Create an aromatherapy relaxation formula by combining essential oils. Either spray into the air or use in a diffuser. If you don't want to bother with blending your own, look for premixed scents with names like "Tranquility" and "Relaxation."
- Brew a cup of herbal tea; then curl up in your most comfortable chair and sip slowly. You can find preblended relaxation teas in almost any supermarket. Otherwise, drink chamomile to soothe your nerves.
- Go to a florist or supermarket that sells fresh flowers and splurge on a bouquet for yourself.
- Go into your workshop and try to build a birdhouse out of whatever scrap wood and hardware are lying around. Make it as ridiculous a dwelling for feathered creatures as possible.
- Soak in a bathtub.
- Give yourself an herbal facial. Premixed masks are readily available these days. Be sure to follow the directions. (Do not leave it on longer just because you're convinced it'll work better if you do.)
- Lie on the couch with a book or Sunday newspaper or stack of magazines you've been meaning to look at and allow yourself to fall asleep as often as you like while trying to read them.
- Supergroom yourself from head to toe (include trimming your nose hairs).
- Schedule yourself for regular therapeutic massages to alleviate depression and promote an overall sense of well-being.
- Cook a pot of vegetable soup from scratch with fresh ingredients, making extra for friends.
- Remake your bed with fresh, clean linens.
- Turn on the music of your choice; then dance wildly in the privacy of your home.

# "A Nice, Hot Bath"

3–5 minutes to prepare
1 serving

There are darned few woes that can't be cured—or at least held at bay—by a nice, hot bath. Soaking in a tub is one of the all-time great suggestions that seasoned sponsors frequently trot out when sponsees are feeling cranky, jittery, overtired, or pissed off. While there is some flexibility with the ingredients, don't skimp on the essentials. If you want to turn this relaxing soak into a cleansing bath, add soap and a quick shower rinse at the end.

Bathtub
2 washcloths
Kitchen timer (optional)
Blow-up pillow with suction cups (optional)
Bath towel
Bathrobe, night clothes, or clean sweat suit
35 gallons of water (approximately)
1 cup Epsom salts or mineral bath salts

One of the following essential oil combinations:

>   3 drops lavender essential oil
>   3 drops clary sage essential oil
>   2 drops bergamot essential oil

or:

>   4 drops sandalwood oil
>   2 drops vanilla
>   2 drops lavender

1/4 cup almond oil or milk as a carrier to help the oils
    disperse (optional)

1 handful moisturizing cream
1 votive candle scented with vanilla or lavender
1 compact disc or audiotape of soothing music

Recommended:

Various artists: *Baroque at Bathtime* (Philips)
Benedictine Monks: *Chant* (Angel)
Sequentia: *Canticles of Ecstacy* (Deutsche Harmonia)
Various artists: *Piano Solos* (Narada)
Enya: *Watermark* (Reprise)
Don Campbell: *Essence* (Spirit Music)

1. Start with a sparkling clean bathtub. Move the shower curtain out of the way. Wet suction cups and stick blow-up pillow to wall at shoulder blade height.
2. With the bathroom door closed, fill tub with water, testing temperature with your hand. It should be significantly warmer than body temperature but not unbearably hot. You want to be able to sit in this water for at least ten minutes without breaking out in a sweat or passing out from the heat.
3. Pour Epsom or bath salts in when tub is one-quarter full. Stir with hand to dissolve.
4. While tub is filling, collect washcloths and towel. Light candle and start music. Start taking off your clothes.
5. Wait until tub is filled before adding essential oils so your skin can benefit from them as much as your olfactory system. Either add drops directly and stir to disperse or blend oils slightly ahead of time in a base of almond oil or milk. If the fragrance seems too intense, open the bathroom door for a minute to let the essence dissipate.

6. Set timer (or time your soak to the music). Turn off overhead lights.

7. Remove the rest of your clothes, carefully step into the tub, and slowly lower your body so you can soak up to your neck. If that's too uncomfortable, sit up and use soaking wet washcloths to keep your upper body wet and warm.

8. Remain in tub for at least ten but no more than twenty minutes. If your fingers get prunelike, you've been soaking too long. While soaking, breathe deeply to realize the aromatherapy benefits of the essential oils. Let the music bathe your mind.

9. When the time is up, drain the bathtub and slowly step out. Pat yourself lightly all over with the towel and slather your still-damp skin with moisturizer.

10. Put on your bathrobe, night clothes, or clean sweat suit and leave the room. If you plan to go immediately to bed, remember to blow out the candle and either turn off the music or let it end automatically. Do not attempt bathroom clean-up for several hours or until the next morning.

☛ Collect, listen to, and swap audiotapes about recovery with other Twelve Steppers. Check the "books on tape" section of your public library; ask around at Twelve Step meetings; order from catalogs that cater to the personal growth and self-discovery market (Sounds True, P.O. Box 8010, Boulder, CO 80306, 1-800-333-9185) or the recovery market (Hazelden, 15251 Pleasant Valley Road, P.O. Box 176, Center City, MN 55012, 1-800-328-9000). Your local bookstore probably has a "books on tape" section. Also check in the back of books by popular recovery authors; many offer taped recordings of their work.

☞ To meet clean and sober people, you'll need to go where clean and sober people go. Generally speaking, this means replacing bars, country-club blowouts, heavy-metal concerts, pool halls, strip joints, casinos, and street corners with things you never in a million years thought you'd try—book discussion groups, adult education programs, community service organizations, museum tours, nature walks, church picnics, and public lectures at the local college.

> "Wherever you go, you take yourself with you!"

Take heart, lots of people have already figured out how to have vibrant, fun lives in recovery. An entirely new social world will open up to you once you become part of a Twelve Step fellowship, and *you* do not have to explore any of this alone.

☞ Before planning a radical geographical or career move, examine your motives. While this may look like the most efficient way to change playmates, playgrounds, and playthings—to shift from the culture of addiction to the culture of recovery—it may instead put you at risk for using again. The stress that comes with even planned disruption may lead you right back to addictive forms of self-soothing. This is particularly true during early recovery. Stay put! Practice living clean, sober, and abstinent where your Twelve Step support is located. Remember Dorothy's post-Oz revelation?

☞ No matter what your addiction, it makes sense to change your patterns for eating meals away from home. In your heart of hearts you know exactly what kind of dining atmosphere contributes to your urge to overeat, use drugs, or drink. These are not safe places for you. Find restaurants without bars or liquor licenses. Make sure the place has a "no smoking" section. Avoid "all you can eat" specials and dessert buffets. Needless to say, you will have to retire your bartending career.

☞ It's after midnight and you're jumping out of your skin. Grab a sheet of paper and start writing. You don't have to generate Pulitzer Prize–winning text. Don't worry about spelling, grammar, or syntax. Write whatever comes to mind in that moment. What stinks? What's scary? What else?

If you can read your handwriting, take a look at what you've written. Now, write yourself into some perspective by chronicling how your life was going before you decided to try this Twelve Step business.

If you really feel like crap, skip these preliminary steps and *immediately start writing a list of no fewer than twenty-five reasons to be grateful.*

☞ *Getting sober and staying in recovery happens at many levels of consciousness.* If you aren't keen on keeping a daily diary of your waking hours, at least keep an occasional journal in which you write down dreams. Dreams provide important clues and are themselves a form of work. Incidentally, it is not unusual for people in all stages of recovery to have vivid ones about using: You're surrounded by a bevy of those adorable little bottles of booze that are sold on airplanes . . . it's snowing blow . . . you've got forks in either hand and the most amazing dessert buffet in front of you. These dreams are often so dramatically realistic that you may wake up feeling agitated, hungover, and convinced you've slipped. Write about it in your journal; then talk about it with your sponsor and at your very next meeting.

> "Gratitude is the street-car to a better attitude."

☞ You don't have to have "eating issues" to have your addiction triggered by certain foods. Some food substances, such as caffeine and sugar, trigger the physiological craving for stimulant drugs and alcohol. Other foods may be so psychologically linked to your addictive substance or activity of choice that you're better off abstaining from them. If you can't imagine eating pizza without a pitcher of beer, stay away from pizza. If you can't imagine drinking a cup of coffee without having a cigarette, quit drinking coffee. If hot dogs and peanuts make you want to head for the track . . . well, you get the point.

☞ Most addicts and alcoholics come to realize that instead of preparing for sleep at night, they would simply pass out. Healthier ways to produce quality, cell-repairing sleep include

- eating tryptophan-rich foods about an hour before bedtime—such as scrambled eggs, a slice or two of turkey, or a big handful of roasted pumpkin seeds. Yes, a mug of warm milk also works, but only if you can tolerate lactose. (If your belly balloons out and you double over with gas pains, you're probably lactose intolerant.)
- listening to soft music, environmental sound recordings, the comforting nothing that emanates from "white noise" machines, or your cat's sweet little nose whistles.
- reducing the mental stimulation that comes with watching late-night television, surfing the Internet at bizarre hours, or reading legal thrillers in bed. If space allows, remove all electronic equipment from your bedroom and develop the habit of reading something inspirational instead.
- creating an evening ritual around prayer or meditation to help you slow down to stillness as you climb into bed.

Even if drugs and alcohol aren't your problem, you're still better off using something else to help you sleep. In addition to producing poor quality sleep, alcohol intensifies snoring and sleep apnea, a condition that leads to high blood pressure and cardiovascular problems.

## Sleep, the Final Frontier

Nightly sleep requirements vary among adults, but seven to ten hours is recommended for "normies." During that time, the body moves in and out of physically healing NREM (nonrapid eye movement) sleep in approximately ninety-minute cycles. This is when the body's metabolism slows down enough to repair daily wear and tear on the whole system. Roughly one-fifth of all slumber time is spent in REM (rapid eye movement) sleep, or dreamland, where a gigunda amount of psychological healing work is accomplished.

Smart money says that you did not keep anything close to regular hours when you were active in your addiction. If the addictive substance itself didn't screw with your circadian rhythms, the activity surrounding it, like avoiding jail or making bail, most assuredly did. Add to that your attempts to jump-start with caffeine plus attempts to catch up by crashing out for a few days in a row, and what you have are sleep patterns that are so hopelessly disrupted that it may take years to get back on the right track.

*In other words, don't be surprised if cleaning up your act brings on a strangely paradoxical combination of insomnia and exhaustion.* In fact, at certain points in your recovery you might wonder if you'll ever sleep again. You'd truly like to pop the next person who says, "No one ever died from lack of sleep," but you don't have the energy. At other junctures you might find yourself wondering if you'll ever wake up long enough to hear someone finish a sentence. Don't worry. It's all normal, and it's all a necessary part of the healing process. Eventually you'll need to establish regular hours for going to sleep and waking up.

Until then, go with the flow. When you can't sleep, get up and read something soothing or listen to calming music. When you do feel yourself going down for what seems like an endless count, don't fight it. Take it on faith that you're working your way out of the nightmare of addiction toward sweeter dreams.

# 2

# Go to Meetings

A few lucky souls experience such an immediate sense of belonging after sitting through their very first Twelve Step meeting that they happily show up for more. And then there's everyone else.

You may be relieved to learn that most newcomers recoil when they hear seasoned members recommending frequent, if not daily, meeting attendance. And to be perfectly honest, it's not at all unusual to hear people who have logged some quality time in a Twelve Step program grousing occasionally about having to go to meetings. They go anyway for one simple reason: Meetings help them stay clean, sober, and abstinent.

"Okay," you may be thinking, "so my addiction is no longer working for me or anyone else around me. But does that mean I have to go sit somewhere and talk about it? Uh, every day?" The answer from those who have managed to accumulate any kind of freedom from addiction is a resounding "yes."

*Regular attendance at Twelve Step meetings is a key feature of this recovery model.* Over time you will discover that meetings, with their promise of anonymity and confidentiality, are extraordinarily safe places to hang out—a heck of a lot safer than street corners, bars, shopping malls, back alleys, casinos, or racetracks!

Meetings are where you get to talk about your internal and

external struggles without fed-up friends and family members rolling their eyes. Meetings are where you hear how others manage to break free from their own addictions. Even if you listen halfheartedly while picking at your cuticles, you're bound to hear your own experience expressed in other people's stories. After a while it will occur to you that there's nothing unique about your situation. There will always be those who have had a smoother ride on the road to recovery, as well as those who have barely survived the collision course. Sooner or later you realize comparisons are useless. You discover that you are, in fact, just like everyone else whose life has been screwed up by addictions and compulsions, a revelation that may actually provide a surprising sense of comfort.

But until you reach this point, you will need to take it on whatever faith you can muster that going to meetings on a regular basis will keep you focused on recovery. The tips in this chapter will help you find meetings, choose the right ones for you, and then sit through them into perpetuity without getting too disgruntled as time passes.

## CHAPTER TIPS

☞ In addition to building a strong foundation for staying clean and sober, *attending ninety meetings in ninety days* allows you to explore a variety of formats so you can eventually develop a personalized meeting list. In fact, try to avoid settling into a schedule of regular meetings until you've fully sampled what's available in your area.

☞ Periodically revisit meetings you removed from your list during the first year or two of recovery. Your needs will shift as your recovery progresses, and meetings that seemed creepy early on have a funny way of becoming just fine over time.

☞ Choose at least one meeting to attend faithfully. Having a "home group" provides the continuity most addicts and alco-

> **"The only meeting you're late for is your first."**

holics need, plus a place to become seen, known, and hopefully more authentic over time. This is the place where you will begin taking on the service commitments so essential to continued recovery (e.g., making coffee, greeting people at the door, speaking, cleaning up after meetings).

In addition, some groups exchange speaking commitments, visit treatment facilities or prisons, and staff the phones at local hotlines. Some sponsors view this as mandatory from the get-go for continued recovery; others take a more moderate view. Your degree of participation will change over time.

☞ As you establish a regular meeting schedule, be sure to include at least one meeting devoted to people telling their stories, one that focuses on studying the Twelve Steps, and one that provides an opportunity to discuss the challenges of recovery with people who have more—and less—time in the program than you.

☞ If you're a member of Alcoholic Anonymous, try to attend at least one meeting that focuses on studying the "Big Book" (*Alcoholics Anonymous*).

☞ Knowing where and when tomorrow's meeting will be is one way to ensure that you will continue to go to meetings.

☞ No time for meetings? Take a minute—or sixty—to calculate how much time you used to spend drinking, using, overeating, smoking, shopping, or gambling. Be sure to include all the time you spent planning, then covering up, these activities. Was it less than one hour per day?

☞ Consider significantly reducing or putting your participation in other activities entirely on hold during your first year of recovery so that you can fully immerse yourself in the recovery process. Can't imagine living a full life

**"First things first."**

without Elk, Lions, or Rotary Club events, Little League coaching, B'nai B'rith, or the church picnic committee? Sort it out by asking yourself this question: Does participating with this group or in this activity support my recovery or distract from my recovery?

☞ Spend some time identifying your patterns of using. For example, did you

- light up a cigarette before rolling out of bed every day?
- live for a cocktail hour that lasted until the next morning?
- reserve major binge/purge eating for weekends?
- spend lunch hours scoring and doing drugs in your employer's rest rooms?

Use this information to create a meeting schedule that specifically interrupts the flow of your habit. *In other words, try to attend meetings during what were prime using times.*

## Meeting Formats

Ever since the early hominids huddled around the campfire to chew the fat—both literally and figuratively—human groups have come together to simply talk. Groups may form to sort through life events, discover personal identity, or explore spiritual frontiers. No matter what the group's stated purpose, magic happens when people honestly "speak Self" to others. Isolation starts to evaporate; separation transforms into belonging; empathy becomes possible; loneliness inevitably passes; consciousness eventually emerges; and community is formed.

Twelve Step fellowship meetings, even ones that focus on one speaker's story, make possible the transformation of body, mind, and spirit for those who attend. The basic meeting structure is the same: Serenity Prayer, announcements, self-introduction of newcomers, content, passing the basket, closing prayer. However, as you will discover in your travels, there are a variety of meeting formats. Creating a "mixed portfolio" of meetings will fulfill different needs at different junctures of your recovery. Your options include:

**Speaker meetings.** Usually open to anyone interested in attending, these meetings provide a showcase for one or a few speakers to tell their personal stories. There is no formal discussion period, but there is usually ample time before and after the meeting (with modest refreshments!) to strike up informal conversations. These meetings give newcomers and outsiders (like friends and family members) an inspiring and instructive view of how Twelve Step programs work. They're great for keeping everyone's memory "green."

**Step meetings.** These meetings are devoted to reading and commenting on the Twelve Steps. Generally closed except to those who consider themselves members of a Twelve Step fellowship, these meetings provide a relatively informal and relaxed atmosphere in which to study the Twelve Steps. Step meetings are essential for anyone committed to actively working a Twelve Step program.

**Special-focus discussion meetings.** Similar to Step meetings in style and tone, these meetings zoom in on a particular topic or theme. Some Alcoholics Anonymous groups, for example, will focus a regular meeting on the "Promises" that appear on pages 83 and 84 of the "Big

Book." Other fellowships may focus on certain pieces of program literature or perhaps exclusively on one of the Steps. Most Twelve Step fellowships try to offer beginners meetings where newcomers can discuss what goes on during early recovery. Regardless of topic, discussion meetings are ideal environments for hearing how others face life events—some of which are incredibly inconvenient and annoying—without launching themselves off the planet.

**Special-interest group meetings.** Despite a strong tradition that emphasizes the commonality of purpose, some meetings are open only to members of special-interest groups (e.g., women, men, lesbians and gay men). There are even unpublicized meetings for professionals like doctors, attorneys, and clergy who feel the need for extra anonymity. While some people are appalled at the emergence of these types of special-interest meetings, others argue that they offer a greater level of safety and comfort for those who attend.

When you're just getting started, a beginners meeting is a great place to ask such burning questions as "How come *she* gets to have a guy sponsor?" After you've accumulated some time, beginners meetings are great reminders of what it was like when you first entered recovery.

☞ Find meetings to attend first thing in the morning and, if possible, on your way home from work. Attending meetings at the endpoints of each day can be very stabilizing, especially during early recovery.

☞ You need only one person other than yourself to have a meeting. Remember, Twelve Step fellowships were created after

Bill Wilson discovered he could keep himself from drinking by talking the night away with another alcoholic. Some of the most powerful meetings happen when there are only a few people in the room.

☞ Try to organize your workday and lunch hour so you can get to a noon meeting. (This is usually easier to manage in large metropolitan areas.)

If there's no noon meeting nearby, set aside part of your lunch hour to read some program literature, make a gratitude list, or call your sponsor (only if you're allowed to make personal calls). The point is to make some kind of contact to keep your recovery on track during work.

☞ Some large corporations, educational institutions, and healthcare facilities sponsor on-site Twelve Step program meetings for staff and inmates. Should you go? Talk through the pros and cons of doing this with your sponsor and trusted friends in the program. In theory, everyone at the meeting is there for the same thing and understands the principle of anonymity. On the other hand, your position may be such that attending relatively public meetings would not be such a swell idea.

> "Relax. You're not going to get it by Thursday."

☞ Wondering where to sit at a meeting? Here are some guidelines:

- Feeling antsy? Sit in the front.
- Easily distracted by friends? Sit in the front.
- Have trouble hearing? Sit in the front.
- Want to stay sober? Sit in the front.
- Still looking for trouble? Sit in the back.

☞ Double or even triple up on meetings when you're especially vulnerable to your addiction. This includes

- feeling weird and wired for no apparent reason (remember, this is when you used to anesthetize yourself)
- being unemployed, underemployed, or otherwise having a lot of unstructured time on your hands
- preparing to leave for an out-of-town trip
- coming up on major calendar events like holidays, anniversaries (especially ones connected with coming into a Twelve Step program), and family get-togethers
- getting rocked by unanticipated, dramatic life events such as disease, death, financial destitution, and employment crises

☞ Switch to different meetings for a while if you develop a crush on one of the other regular attendees. There are no other meetings? Then seat yourself so the subject of your desire is obscured from view. If you're married, keep your eyes on your wedding band and your ears open to the speaker.

☞ Granted, this isn't always possible in small towns, but if you can, make sure you attend different meetings from your intimate partner, spouse, or mere housemate who is also in the program. This is especially important early on when everyone, without exception, is quick to blame others for almost everything but the weather.

☞ Plan out-of-town meeting attendance when you're scheduled to travel. It doesn't matter whether you're on vacation, visiting relatives, or traveling for business. Being away from home is particularly stressful and distracting for people in recovery. Take care of yourself by taking the following actions:

• Call ahead of time to find out where your Twelve Step fellowship meets.
• Arrange for someone to pick you up and take you to meetings.
• Announce in the meeting that you're visiting from out of town and how long you'll be around.
• Get local phone numbers. This is important if you've traveled to another time zone and would be waking up your buddies at home at strange, inconvenient hours.

☞ If you're staying at a hotel, you'll need to give your last name to the local contact person so that he or she can call you back. Most hotel switchboards will not put incoming calls through without this complete information.

☞ Adopt an attitude of curiosity about the regional differences you encounter at meetings away from home. The fundamentals—like the entire point of meeting in the first place—will remain the same wherever you attend, despite differences in format. At some meetings, speakers wait to be called on by the leader. In others, the floor belongs to whomever starts talking first. You may find yourself at a meeting where everyone in the room speaks in turn or at one where everyone sits in candlelit silence after reciting the Serenity Prayer. In other words, don't be surprised if the meeting you attend isn't exactly like your regular meetings at home. Use this time to practice acceptance.

☞ If you travel to the same place frequently for business, establish yourself as a regular at an out-of-town meeting. You might want to also ask someone to be a temporary sponsor in that locale if work responsibilities require you to spend weeks or months away from home.

☞ Today's electronic technology makes it easy to attend meetings if and when you can't get out of the house. With a computer and modem, you can easily connect to other Twelve Steppers either through one of the commercial on-line groups (e.g., CompuServe, America Online) or by surfing the Internet. Key search word: Recovery. (See appendix C for some Internet recovery addresses.)

**"Meeting makers make it."**

☞ If you're traveling and can't find a meeting of your particular Twelve Step fellowship, look up "AA" or "Alcoholics Anonymous" in the phone book, call the local Intergroup, and find an "open" AA meeting. These are meetings anyone may attend. In addition to being the mother of all Twelve Step programs, Alcoholics Anonymous meets all over the world and is relatively easy to find. Remember, though, that the meeting will be focused on recovery from alcoholism. Still, any Twelve Step meeting is better than none if you're feeling at risk.

☞ Good resources for finding meetings include local hospitals, social workers specializing in addictions, spiritual advisors, clergy, and family-practice-oriented physicians.

One ultimate source for information is the telephone book. Most directories include numbers for addiction information and referral services under "emergency number" listings right in the front. And don't forget, you can always call directory assistance.

☞ If you are struggling with addiction as well as an emotional or psychiatric illness, try to find at least one meeting for people with "dual disorders." Such meetings, which are usually found at treatment centers, are extremely helpful for learning about how to work a Twelve Step program of recovery while being treated within the mental health system.

☞Multiple addictions? (Welcome to the club!) Choose *one* Twelve Step fellowship as your primary program. Get anchored in that one first by going to meetings, finding a sponsor, and working the Steps to provide the foundation you'll need before tackling your other addictions.

☞Even if you don't particularly feel like sharing at a meeting, you can participate by simply stating who and what you are. There's tremendous healing power in raising your hand to say, "Hi. My name is . . . and I am a . . . " out loud to a group of kindred souls. *Sharing is the first step to ending the isolation of addiction.*

By the way, you can sit in meeting rooms for years without sharing anything more than this and still realize benefits from listening and working the Twelve Steps with a sponsor.

☞Tailor your sharing to whatever addiction is the focus of the Twelve Step meeting you're attending.

☞Keep your sharing at meetings brief and to the point, i.e., about recovering from addiction. Try to avoid waxing eloquent about the gruesome details of your personal problems unless you sincerely believe they are immediately putting you at risk for drinking, drugging, smoking, overeating, gambling, and the like.

Although sharing uninterrupted in a group has therapeutic value, Twelve Step fellowship meetings were never intended to be a substitute for formal, professionally facilitated group therapy.

By the way, as therapeutic experiences go, Twelve Step programs offer quite a good deal. The meetings last a full hour and are free, although a buck or two in the basket is what keeps the program going. (In AA, this is called the Seventh Tradition, which states that the group must be self-supporting. So do your bit—it's still a bargain at many, many times the price.)

☞ Unless it's the custom and style of the meeting to mention anniversary dates before sharing—or it is legitimately your anniversary—don't do it. Why not? There are two very good reasons. First, everyone in every Twelve Step program theoretically has the same amount of time: today. Second, it rarely comes across as anything other than boastful.

Once you've accumulated some time, it's more appropriate to make modest reference to the fact with such phrases as:

- After coming around a while . . .
- Having accumulated a few twenty-fours . . .
- When I first came into recovery . . .

☞ Feeling really nervous about piping up in meetings where you might be recognized? Keep the following factors in mind:
- No one takes attendance.
- You never have to fill out a membership form.
- Everyone else is there for the same reason.
- Most people are so focused on themselves they're not paying super-duper attention to you.
- Last names aren't used, so unless your first name is really odd, there is probably at least one other person in the room with the same name.
- You can always find meetings in another town.

☞ It's a good idea to attend meetings on those days you absolutely, positively don't want to because you think you're cured, feel bored with the whole clean scene, believe you've figured it all out, or find everyone and everything stupid beyond belief. Heard frequently at Twelve Step meetings is the suggestion to "Keep coming until you want to keep coming." This may happen suddenly or take quite a while.

Alternatively, you may embrace the whole process of getting

sober, adore meetings, and love the people at them. This is
what's known as being on a "pink
cloud," and this euphoria can last for
years before the rude awakening happens. Another bit of Twelve Step wis-
dom is this: First it gets better, then it gets worse, then it gets
different, and then it gets real.

> **"Keep bringing your body and your mind will follow."**

☛ Join a speaker meeting that actively exchanges with other
groups if you tend to isolate or otherwise keep to yourself. This
will help you overcome your fear of people and social situations.
(This "suggestion" to join a speaker meeting was practically
considered a requirement at one point.)

☛ Unless you're at a closed meeting where you know everyone, try to share as if there's a scared, confused newcomer in the
room who needs a dose of hope. Chances are that person is there.

## Go Right Ahead, Laugh and Cry. It's Good for You!

Many Twelve Step fellowship meetings and those of
Alcoholics Anonymous in particular include an unexpected and incredibly high level of hilarity. Newcomers
are generally stunned by the frequent bursts of laughter.
A fiercely independent soul suddenly needs rides after
knee surgery; a hyper-diligent workaholic is laid off; the
dating scene falls apart for someone with under a year of
recovery. All this and more is shared, and the whole room
cracks up laughing. "What *are* these people laughing at?"
mutters the newcomer. The answer? Themselves.

This ability to see, then express, the laugh-out-loud
humor of stressful circumstances turns out to have major
health benefits. There are lots of reasons why laughter is

considered the best medicine. Psychologists and psychiatrists who study laughter have found that it strengthens the immune system, lowers blood pressure, releases tension, boosts energy, enhances alertness and memory, contributes to longevity, and facilitates positive mood shifts.

As it turns out, crying also provides terrific health and beauty benefits. Researchers who study this end of the emotional spectrum laud crying as a natural means of body detoxification. Emotional tears differ chemically from those resulting from eye irritation. They're higher in protein, beta-endorphins which reduce pain, prolactin, and ACTH (adrenocorticotropic hormone, another indicator of stress released by the pituitary gland). Crying, then, washes away whatever harmful chemicals the body produces in response to stress and restores the body to equilibrium. Like laughing, crying lowers blood pressure and reduces emotional, as well as muscular, tension. And it doesn't seem to matter whether the crying is in response to sadness, happiness, anger, sympathy, anxiety, or fear. Any or all of these emotions may make an appearance during a Twelve Step meeting. Crying is not only the healthy thing to do, but it's great for your skin!

☛ Sick and tired of hearing the same people share the same stories over and over again? Since recovery is a lifelong process

> **"Take what you want and leave the rest."**

and Twelve Step programs are steeped in an oral tradition, repetition is unavoidable. Stuff gets repeated a lot, so you may as well get used to it. Remember, your meeting mates are sick and tired of hearing your story too!

Make a conscious effort to discover something new in what is being said, or switch meetings for a while. You'll hear what are essentially the same stories, but because they're emanating from different people, you'll hear them differently.

☞ Addicts, even those with some recovery time, are known for being "restless, irritable, and discontented" with almost no provocation. If you have a reputation for huffing off when things don't go exactly your way, think twice before switching meetings. Staying put and turning the whole scene over to a Higher Power may be the more sober thing to do.

☞ Whenever you encounter a speaker who seems to be making absolutely no sense, listen to the feelings being expressed rather than the words being used to express them. Scan the room and notice other people's reactions. You're guaranteed to find at least one person nodding enthusiastically. This, incidentally, is an excellent way to cultivate a more generous spirit.

☞ *Listening is a lot easier if you focus on identifying rather than comparing your experience with that of whomever is speaking.* What does this mean? You're getting

> **"Learn to listen so that you can listen to learn."**

caught up in comparisons if—in your head—you're saying, "Heck, I ate (or drank, drugged, gambled away) much more (or less) than *that* person." Take it as a given that you can always find someone who made much more (or much less) of a mess than you did.

Your chances of accepting your addiction and staying sober increase when you are able to appreciate other people's stories as a way of life that didn't work—either for them or you.

☞ Prevent personal resentments from spinning out of control by unobtrusively leaving the room when people who bug you are speaking. Go freshen up your cup of coffee. Visit the bathroom. You always have the option of sticking around and pondering what's being triggered in you, but it's better to leave and do the pondering elsewhere if you're visibly seething.

☞ Don't worry about nodding off for a nap during meetings. This is actually a good thing. It means you're finally beginning to relax, and you won't miss anything because everything being shared will enter subliminally.

☞ Counting clean days? Musing about using booze, drugs, gambling, or whatever? Dreaming about this jazz at night? Be sure to raise your hand to announce this at the beginning of each meeting. Sharing your thoughts about using is especially important if you're new to recovery or are returning after another dip into addiction. Not only does this activity keep you honest, but it lets others know you need more support.

☞ Try to reserve judgment about other people, the quality of their recovery, how they behave in meetings, and what they share when they speak. You will be amazed at how wonderfully wise some people start sounding as you become more sober. The reverse is also true. Don't be too surprised if the people you idolized early on seem like ordinary, flawed human beings after you've been around them for a while.

☞ If you have trouble getting it together to make meetings on time, try one of the following techniques:

• Sign up to make the coffee.
• Ask someone for a ride.
• Offer someone a ride.
• Agree to meet someone at the meeting.

☞ Listening at meetings is as essential as sharing. Paying attention is so centrally important that the Twelve Step oral tradition is filled with such charming aphorisms as "Shut up" and "Take the cotton out of your ears and stick it in your mouth."

Still, you might find it challenging to concentrate on what others are saying, especially at the beginning when everything is fuzzy. Help focus your attention by occupying your hands:

- Doodle on a small piece of paper.
- Use a Styrofoam cup for your coffee and cut elaborate designs into it with your thumbnail.
- Shred a cigarette instead of smoking it.
- Engage in any of the portable needle crafts like knitting, crocheting, or embroidery.

Note: Keep your movements quiet and circumspect out of regard for the group.

☞ Avoid leading meetings until you've acquired some time—at least ninety days. (In some fellowships, newcomers cannot lead meetings until they've made it past the ninety-day mark.) It may look as if there's nothing to it, but—in fact—a different level of concentration is required to lead a meeting. It is, for example, sometimes more difficult to listen carefully because leading involves responding to raised hands. However, some meetings do seem to run themselves, and all the leader does is open and close it with announcements, readings, and prayers. Even if this is the type of meeting you attend, hold off on leading for a while. You're better off focusing your full attention on gleaning morsels of wisdom from what's being said.

## There Are No Rules, but There Is Etiquette

Twelve Step fellowships make a big deal out of the fact that there are no rules, just suggestions for behavior. Since most addicts are stunningly selfish, self-absorbed, and otherwise out of it—especially during early recovery—meetings are where many learn the value of good manners. Here are a few top tips for meeting etiquette:

**Be on time**. Meetings start and end promptly. They usually last an hour. Sometimes being late is unavoidable, but something else is undoubtedly going on if you consistently wander in after the meeting begins or skip out before it's over. If you share in the meeting after arriving late, develop the habit of apologizing to the group for your lateness. This serves multiple purposes. It prevents you from pretending you're on time, cultivates sensitivity for others, and provides practice for making amends in the future.

**Speak for yourself.** What you say needs to be based on your own experience as someone in recovery. Cross-talk, where you either subtly or blatantly comment on someone else's sharing, is considered very bad form. Needless to say, muttering opinions under your breath to the person sitting next to you isn't cool either.

**Thank speakers.** Using the phrase "Thank you for sharing" is yet another attempt to instill courtesy in people for whom such sensitivity to others has been sorely lacking for years. When it's your turn during discussion meetings, remember to thank previous speakers. This doesn't have to be elaborate. "I want to thank everyone for sharing so far" is sufficient. After speaker meetings, try to get to the point where you automatically get off your butt to personally give the speaker(s) a hearty handshake and word of thanks.

## Uh, Do I Hafta?

And then there are those meeting components that have become an integral part of Twelve Step custom and tradition. Because these features are essential, they may appear to be mandatory. They're not. No, you don't have to partake in any of the following customs:

**Pray out loud.** It doesn't seem to matter how often people say Twelve Step fellowships have nothing to do with religion. People still get confused and cranky, especially if the meeting begins with a short version of the Serenity Prayer and ends with Christianity's central prayer, the Lord's Prayer. This drill flips some people out and offends others. You don't have to recite the prayers. You don't even have to look remotely pious. Simply stand there, breathe, and feel grateful to be alive.

**Contribute money.** As mentioned earlier, Twelve Step fellowships have a Seventh Tradition of being financially self-supporting through contributions from members. The money goes for meeting-space rent, coffee, cookies, and sometimes a contribution to the next level of group fellowship. If you feel uncomfortable contributing money to a particular meeting, you don't have to put a buck in the basket.

**Hold hands.** Somewhere along the line, someone came up with the idea of everyone holding hands to recite stuff at the end of the meeting. In some places, this is followed by a little hand squeeze and the words "Keep coming back. It works if you work it." If this ritual gives you the creeps or strikes you as massively unhygienic, you don't have to hang onto someone else's paw. You don't have to hug anyone, either.

☞ Stay put in a meeting until you hear something you need to hear, even if that something is "We have a nice way of closing."

☞ Reduce feelings of awkwardness and not fitting in by getting active in a group. If you're shy, volunteer for behind-the-scenes stuff like making coffee and cleaning up. Alternatively, since the whole idea is to change your life, do the exact opposite of what you'd be most inclined to do. Become a greeter at the door if you're shy. Volunteer to do something unobtrusive yet necessary like wiping tables or stacking chairs if you've tended to be a big backslapper in the past.

☞ Anniversary meetings are wonderful sources of inspiration. Some groups celebrate members' anniversaries at the end of each month. Others have people celebrating almost every week. Groups will also throw anniversary parties to celebrate the durability of a particular meeting; the party may include hosting a special speaker and providing food. Any and all of these celebrations are a great way to see how working a Twelve Step program works over time. They're also an opportunity to learn how to party without drugs or alcohol.

By the way, be sure to publicly celebrate your anniversary when it finally comes around. Announcing how many twenty-four hours you've put together provides an enormous source of hope for others.

# 3

## Reaching Out

Most active addicts stink at relationships.

Not you, of course. You were always the proverbial life of the party. Your pithy observations about everything and nothing made you a much-sought-after dinner guest. During family holidays, you had all the kids squealing with joy while their parents—your stuffy siblings—looked on with disgust. When it came to pitching new business, you were without a doubt the firm's silver-tongued savior. You had a wide circle of friends who would do anything for you—as long as you were buying. Never mind that as your addiction progressed, invitations anywhere started to dwindle. Come to think of it, your boss was none too pleased about that hearty barrage of tasteless jokes you told during a key client conference.

Right before hitting bottom, you hid out at home—remote control in one hand and your favorite (or most easily procured) mood-altering substance gripped in the other. Nothing pathological about your slow retreat from the world of relationships. What was everyone bitching about? You were just feeling introspective, needing some space from mere mortals. To hell with the idiot boss who hauled you in for an attitude adjustment, the nosy sister who kept asking if you were okay, and the rat bastards who deserted you when the money ran out. Ask for help? Why bother? Nothing was wrong, and even if it was, no one could possibly appreciate your special, sensitive nature.

Yep, you stunk at relationships. It only took trying to manage life without using and abusing a social lubricant of some sort for you to realize this. Shocked to discover your inability to either fit in or stand out, you wanted to return to the perceived safety of addiction. But now you're trying a Twelve Step program and have nixed that option. What's a recovering addict to do? *Learn* how to reach out to others.

Here's the good news: Twelve Step fellowships offer a relatively safe environment for acquiring and practicing relational skills. Attend meetings regularly, and you'll learn how to speak and listen more carefully. Participate in fellowship-related activities, and you'll encounter ample opportunities to practice such innovative behaviors as generosity, honesty, and humility.

More good news: You won't be doing all this growing up alone. You'll be surrounded by others who are either struggling with the same stuff or have already successfully wrestled with their own social incompetence. In either event, you'll have lots of room to bumble along, for a while anyway. Eventually, you'll learn how to be around others—in and out of program—without feeling that desperate need to hide in plain sight.

Use the tips in this chapter as a guide to your reentry into the world of relationships. Hopefully, you will quickly discover that talking with a sponsor, cultivating friendships, and reaching out in a healthier way is an essential feature of recovery. This chapter also provides handy hints for dealing with problems whose solutions lie way beyond the considerable talents of your recovery chums.

## CHAPTER TIPS

☞ When choosing a sponsor, do your heart, psyche, and soul a big favor and select someone whose personality traits seem to be exactly opposite of your parents. Raised with a lot of harsh verbal criticism? Then choose a sponsor who, in addition to solid recovery, has a tender heart and gentle delivery. If you ruled the family roost and strutted all over your parents, choose a sponsor who takes a disciplined, no-nonsense approach to working the Twelve Steps.

☞ In addition to serving as your personal tour guide through "Recoveryland," your sponsor will essentially function as your conscience until you manage to develop one. For this, your first real relationship in recovery, you'll need to choose someone of the same sex. After all, you don't want to totally (and literally) screw up your fledgling attempts at recovery by falling in love— or lust—with him or her.

If you're *not* heterosexual, choose a sponsor of the same sex who is absolutely, totally, completely, without-a-shadow-of-a-doubt ineligible for any hanky-panky because he or she *is* heterosexual (yet not homophobic) or devoid of any physical characteristics that you shallowly believe (until you're more sober, of course) make for a meaningful relationship.

What if you're the only woman or man in the group? Okay, go ahead and choose a sponsor of the opposite sex but no one you'd ever have the hots for.

## Watch Out! Don't Trip on That Thirteenth Step

Sooner or later, you will hear people snidely referring to a thirteenth step that shows up nowhere in official program literature. The vibrational field around these comments will feel odd, perhaps even secretive—kind of like catching your elders talking about kinky sex, which is exactly what they're doing.

Thirteenth stepping is program code for "hitting on a newcomer" or, more delicately put, "inappropriate sexual conduct."

Yes, despite all the highfalutin' talk of ethics, integrity, safety, and spirituality in Twelve Step fellowships, some people nevertheless specialize in becoming emotionally and sexually intimate with those who, by virtue of having not a heck of a lot of time in recovery, are vulnerable to these attentions.

Initially, these liaisons look fairly innocent and somewhat romantic, feeding into every addict's secret fantasies of rescuing and being rescued. But because these entanglements involve major disparities of emotional power if not health, under closer scrutiny they look . . . tangled. And, lest you jump to the conclusion that this is some sexist thing that the boys do, be assured that it is not; women have been known to prey on confused, needy newcomers as well.

If, when you are relatively new (i.e., up to at least two years of continuous clean time), you suddenly become the object of total fascination and devotion for someone with way more time than you have, do not feel flattered. Instead, walk away. Quickly. Without tripping on the notorious thirteenth step.

☞ Before asking someone to sponsor you, find out who sponsors *that* person. Now, take a good long look at your potential lineage. Is your "grandsponsor" still going to meetings and working the Steps? Or is that person a phantasm, nowhere to be seen or heard?

When your sponsor has a sponsor, you can relax, knowing that the person onto whom you've unloaded your travails is in turn unloading his or hers onto someone else. In the Twelve Step world, you-know-what really does flow upstream. Needless to say, avoid people who think *you* absolutely need a sponsor but *they* absolutely do not.

☞ To the extent that you can figure this out, make a list of what you think you need from a sponsor (e.g., regular face-to-face contact, lots of guidance and homework for working the Steps, someone who'll sit next to you at a meeting). This will help minimize the possibility of linking up with someone whose sponsoring style won't work for you. At the same time, be open to the very real possibility that it'll take a couple of years for you to figure out what will and won't work for you.

> "You alone can do it, but you can't do it alone."

☞ Call your sponsor while you're really steamed about something that happened. Reporting events, feelings, and reactions in real time is bound to reveal some of the "shortcomings" you'll be wanting to handle eventually by working Steps Six and Seven. Calling in a pitched frenzy will help your sponsor better serve you.

☞ While e-mail is no substitute for live contact, it's a great way to stay in touch with your sponsor—or other program pals— if you travel a lot or have an otherwise extremely busy schedule that messes with your meeting attendance.

Be supersensitive about honoring the long-standing tradition of anonymity if you send e-mail to or receive it at an office. While Twelve Step programs are generally held in high regard by human resource folks, the fact that you and your cyber–pen pal are in recovery is best kept private.

☞ Respect, not friendship, is a prerequisite for sponsorship. Choose someone who has something you want—long-term sobriety, an aura of serenity, a strong faith in a Higher Power, or an ability to take life in stride. You'll discover this by listening and observing carefully at meetings and fellowship-related functions.

If your sponsor morphs into a friend over time, swell, but you're probably better off keeping that relationship distinct—at least in the beginning. This is especially important if you have a history of avoiding authority and accountability or of trying to circumvent it by becoming chummy with and cleverly co-opting whoever might be in a position to call you on your stuff.

☞ How many sponsors? There's no law that says you may have only one, and it certainly can seem more efficient to have a bevy of sponsors—specialists, as it were. You might find someone you really want to sponsor you who, because of his or her own responsibilities and obligations, is not available after 10:00 P.M. or on weekends. You may be gamely—against all best advice—working your way through a couple of Twelve Step programs simultaneously and feel the need for the perspective of a sponsor-type in each. Or you may be on the verge of running (yet another) con game.

It's in your very best interest to do some honest soul-searching before setting up a sponsoring "dream team." If "getting over" was your favorite sport in the bad old days and nights of your addiction, limit yourself to one sponsor so you can't play one against another . . . or two . . . or three.

☞ Choosing a temporary sponsor is a great solution if you

- want a trial period to see whether you really are ready and, even more important, willing to be sponsored by that particular person
- have asked someone to sponsor you who is not available until some time in the future
- are brand new to recovery and haven't been to many meetings—yet
- think that no matter what anyone says, you personally don't need a sponsor because you're so special

Make sure you and your temporary sponsor have a real live conversation (as opposed to one in your head) during which you *mutually* agree upon a time period for the trial relationship. After the period is up, you'll both decide whether to continue the relationship or move on. Remember, "Expectations are resentments waiting to happen."

## Your Sponsor Is a Keeper If He or She . . .

- Requests that you make frequent, even daily, contact at the beginning of your journey through Recoveryland or at times when you're bumbling through something major.
- Is either available at any time for anything that you alone might consider an emergency or sets and keeps very clear boundaries about when and if to call.
- Leaves messages on your answering machine kindly reminding you to "call your sponsor" if you disappear from meetings and stop calling.
- Consistently makes suggestions that tick you off, such as:
    - "Double up on your meetings."
    - "Write out a gratitude list."
    - "Volunteer to make coffee."
    - "Pray."
- Insists that you use the Twelve Steps—especially the first three—to work through difficult situations and the feelings they invariably trigger.
- Drags you off to speaking commitments in public with other people in recovery instead of letting you stew in your own juices at home.
- Won't let you whine, complain, or blame other people and external circumstances for making you have to enter a Twelve Step program of recovery.

## Feel Free to Fire Your Sponsor If He or She . . .

- Doesn't return phone calls for more than two days in a row.
- Can't be bothered to attend more than one meeting a week.
- Uses sharing time in meetings (or at the "meeting after the meeting") to trash the Twelve Steps, the fellowship, and everyone in it.
- Isn't involved in any service work like leading meetings, greeting people at the door, sharing at meetings, or helping to clean up.
- Has a zillion other sponsees and can't quite get it together to meet with you.
- Talks incessantly about self without linking it to something you're currently facing in recovery.
- Thinks the Twelve Steps can be done haphazardly, out of order.
- Has a relapse or seems to be well on the way to having one.

☛ Wait at least forty-eight hours before firing your sponsor, especially for saying stuff you absolutely do not want to hear and for making stupid suggestions. Use this time to mull over the radical notion that he or she may be right.

☛ Early on, make a point of hanging out near (if not actually with) people who have considerably more time in recovery than you. Spending time with long-timers will bolster your sense of hope, even if you can't understand what the heck they're talking about. Just notice if they seem "joyous, happy, and free," or at least not totally bonkers.

As you get more acclimated to sober living, start hanging out with people who have less time than you do in the program. Spending time with newcomers, especially anyone who has just arrived and is rubbed raw by life, will help you remember the pain of hitting your own physical, emotional, and/or spiritual bottom(s).

☞ Make a special effort to stay connected with others in your "recovery cohort"—that group of people who started getting clean and sober around the same time you did. It doesn't matter whether someone arrived via a rehab, a counselor's suggestion, as a result of a spousal ultimatum, or walked in "off the street." The process of recovery shares enough unifying features to make this cohort one of great importance to you.

These are the people you'll want to call for reality checks as you travel the stations of recovery together. And while it is true that all of you may indeed have distorted perceptions about what sobriety is supposed to be like, at least they'll be *shared* distortions.

## Nobody Knows the Troubles I've Seen/Hosanna

Singing the blues? Keep it in the rooms of your recovery fellowship; warble it into your sponsor's ear. Spare the "civilians" in your life—those friends, family members, and work colleagues who have been watching you self-destruct for years.

Shouting for joy? Hold off on any major dramatic announcements of your salvation and healing until you've worked at least the first seven Steps and have made observable, quantifiable, and sustained behavior changes.

Yes, recovery is the greatest thing that ever happened to you. Yes, it's the greatest thing to hit your circle of loved ones. But your primary job is to stay stopped, go to meetings, and work the Steps while they, your loved ones, cycle through feeling numb, relieved, and really quite peeved about what they've been through.

☛ See yourself as others see you! Program wisdom has it that everything screeched to a halt the year you became active in your addiction. If you started sniffing glue at age eight, you're basically stuck there. Didn't have your first drink until you pledged a college fraternity? You undoubtedly have the mindset of an eighteen-year-old. Waited until you were making some bucks before indulging in cocaine? Okay, so you're a twenty-five-year-old trapped in a middle-aged body.

Whatever your situation, just take it for granted that you're a prime example of arrested development. In all likelihood you don't/can't/won't see this about yourself. Getting to know other people who became active at the same age as you did can, therefore, be very revealing—and instructive. After all, if you think *they're* immature . . .

☛ Hate making telephone calls? Dread the mere thought of someone simply saying "Hello" at the other end? No problem. Call when you are most likely to get voice mail or answering machines. Sooner or later you're going to realize the emotional and spiritual value of reaching out. Talking to answering machines first allows you to practice safely for this happy day.

And if calling the answering machines of people who might know you (never mind that you're both in an anonymous program) is a total freak-out, practice using the phone by calling the local organization that serves people with your addiction and talking anonymously to an anonymous telephone volunteer.

Still too close to home? Okay, call one of these organizations in a neighboring state. From a phone booth. Whatever. *Just practice lifting the phone and asking for help.*

☞ Remember to leave your name, phone number, a time to call you back, and, if you don't yet know the person you're calling, some basic identifying information:

> "Hi, I'm Suzy Q., the tall, nervous blond with glasses and lots of earrings from the Tuesday night nonsmoking, open, speaker-discussion Step meeting in the basement of the church where they have cheese and crackers in addition to really bad coffee and cheap cookies."

**"Loneliness is curable."**

Also, if it doesn't really matter whether you get a callback in a timely manner, be sure to say so:

"I'd appreciate a callback, but if you don't have time that's okay because it's not really an emergency, and I just called ten other people on my list anyway."

☞ You've finally mustered the guts to not only pick up the telephone, but dial it. Oh dear, someone has actually answered. Now what? You don't ever have to worry about what to say if, after your initial greeting, you ask, "How are you doing?"

Self-absorption is a key feature of addictive personalities, and most folks are only too happy to yak incessantly about themselves. Listen carefully to whatever data tumbles out. It's a good guess that your stuff may look just like theirs at some point.

☞ Become a decent member of recovery society by practicing phone etiquette during your calls to program people. Learn, then use any or all of these handy phrases at the beginning and end of your phone conversations:

- "Is this a good time for us to talk?"
- "I have to unload; do you have the energy to listen?"

- "How much time can you spend listening to me now?"
- "Thanks for the suggestions."
- "I appreciate your spending this time with me."

☞ You're allowed to whine if it'll prevent you from slipping, but put parameters around the self-pity fetes. Give yourself half an hour, half a day, or half your phone list to be bent out of shape. If you suspect you're incapable of monitoring your own moaning, tell the person on the receiving end, "Don't let me whimper about this for more than ten minutes."

☞ Advanced phone etiquette:
- If what you have to say ends up being more complex and time-consuming than you had thought, interrupt yourself long enough to ask whether you should continue or set up another time to call or meet.
- Call back to provide a brief status report about what happened as a result of their being there for you.

☞ You've finally gotten into the necessary habit of attending regular Twelve Step meetings. Now be prepared to set aside an equivalent amount of time to make program phone calls, especially on days when you miss (or skip!) meetings. Keep in mind that it's useful to organize these calls so that you have a chance to touch base with the emissaries of your new reality throughout the day.

☞ The quickest, most efficient way to get phone numbers is to
- announce that you're new to the program/area/particular meeting and that you need phone numbers
- pass a copy of the meeting list or a blank sheet of paper around at meetings for people to sign (remember to

write your name at the top so that only women or only
men sign up as appropriate)

Once you get the list back, annotate it so you can connect names
with faces. Also note who can be called at the crack of dawn or
late at night. Keep a copy in your wallet, briefcase, backpack, or
purse; another copy by your phone.

☞ The names on your phone list will change as you not only
listen to what and how people share, but observe how their lives

> **"If you share your pain,
> you cut it in half; if you
> don't, you double it."**

seem to be going. *Over time, you may
discover a disquieting disconnect between what people say and what they
actually do.* Humans! But try not to
make (too many) judgments about the quality of another person's
program.

Even if you do, try to avoid completely erasing names and
numbers from your list. You never know who might save your
life or, less dramatically, be able to give you a ride to the supermarket when your car is at the repair shop.

☞ Be sure to learn the last names of key people on your phone
list so that you can look their number up if you get stranded
somewhere without your list. (The anonymity thing does not
mean you can't know the last names of people in the rooms. It
means *they* decide whether or not to reveal this information.)

☞ At some point, start acquiring the names and numbers of
people who work in the same industry or have the same kind of
job responsibilities as you. Reach out to these people when you
find yourself feeling agitated about work-related situations.
Some major corporations, educational institutions, and govern-
ment agencies actually host on-site Twelve Step meetings.

☛ People give you the jitters, but you're starving for connection. What's an addict to do? Consider working your way up the evolutionary scale of relating to others by starting with a pet.

Begin with low- or no-maintenance creatures like fish or turtles. Hold off on mice, gerbils, or hamsters until the hustle and bustle between your ears has slowed down. These furry critters are entirely too frenetic for someone whose goal is more serenity.

If you want slavish, mostly mute devotion and don't at all mind incessant demands for play, go the dog route. When you're ready to practice setting and keeping boundaries, let yourself be adopted by a cat.

☛ In addition to a sponsor, call at least four other people on a regular basis—almost daily if you (and they) can stand it. These are the folks who will form the core of your "support group." Like your sponsor, these people will be more savvy about what's happening in your personal life than those you see only at meetings. Consequently, they will

> "Friends are God's apology for your family."

- have a more comprehensive and accurate context for listening to how you slug through—or avoid—daily life events
- be better able to hold you accountable for your (mis)behaviors
- rally around if you start slipping and sliding your way to a relapse
- provide an instant short list of people to call for feedback before making any major snap decisions like leasing a new car, getting a tattoo, or going on a month-long juice fast to lose weight even though you're in recovery for an eating disorder

# To Call or Not to Call?
## Understanding the Question

Addicts are not exactly known for having incredible powers of discernment. You will frequently hear people with any kind of accumulated time in a Twelve Step fellowship confess, "My best thinking got me here." This is a witty way of admitting that a slew of what seemed to be fabulous decisions and terrific life plans only continued the inexorable downward spiral of addiction.

This *stunning lack of perception about Self* and inability to judge what is important follows some folks into recovery like a bloodhound on a scent.

Recovering addicts have a tendency toward emotional dyslexia: They will get positively hysterical over nothing, while downplaying or ignoring what any so-called normal person would consider a major crisis. At the same time, it's a pretty well-established pseudo-fact that addicts will slide away from recovery over virtually anything. Therefore, no event is too little, petty, annoying, or ridiculous to discuss. The issue is primarily one of timing.

Here are some simple guidelines about when to pick up the phone at an ungodly hour to ask for support.

Do not hesitate to call, if you

- feel like using or have decided you're cured and so fully recovered that you can experiment with having just one (fill in the blank)
- find yourself in a crisis involving something medical like profuse bleeding, broken bones poking through the skin, uncontrollable puking, breathtaking pain, or a fever so high you could fry eggs on your forehead
- get caught up in a continuous loop of volatile emotions, like a major gut-wrenching crying jag, the urge to run

away from everyone and everything, or uncontrollable giddiness
- suddenly have to deal with a situation that could jeopardize your recovery, such as being summarily fired, getting unexpected news about terminal illness or death, or winning a zillion bucks in the lottery

Take nothing and call in the morning, if you
- can't decide whether to go to medical school, drive a truck, or become a beautician
- suddenly realize that your aging parents have no short-term memory, and you absolutely do not want to spend next year's holidays with them—or any of your siblings, for that matter
- discover that your roommate/spouse/partner/ kid borrowed your favorite outfit and has returned it with what looks to be ketchup smears, maybe blood
- decide that you despise your boss, desperately want a puppy, would look much better as a blond, need cosmetic surgery, or think it's about time you moved to San Francisco

☞ Plan ahead for major holidays, especially ones that traditionally involve lots of family activities, food, alcohol, and extend into agonizingly long four-day weekends.

If you're home, keep your regular meeting and activities schedule. If you're away from home and things start careening out of control, call your friends and sponsor at home to get grounded.

☞ When you reach out for help on a specific issue, make sure you reach out to people who have dealt with that issue after having worked the program for a while. If, for example, you're looking down the barrel of a life-threatening illness, you're probably better off getting advice from someone with four years in recovery who has stayed clean and sober during a course of chemotherapy than from a long-timer with twenty years who has experienced nothing more ominous than a head cold.

☞ Everything will look, sound, and feel different after you start working a program of recovery—birthdays, picnics, weddings, bar mitzvahs, dinners out, movies, dating, dancing, dental visits, and so on. Without chemical support of any kind, you may be shocked to find yourself suddenly clueless about what you like and don't like, what you can or cannot handle.

Talk with others about these "first-time-while-sober events." At least one other person will have had a "first" family vacation, out-of-town business trip, or visiting in-laws experience in recovery that will help you survive yours.

### Are You Married?

Embedded in the text of Step Twelve in one of the sacred texts of Alcoholics Anonymous, *The Twelve Steps and Twelve Traditions,* is this literary gem: "Most married folks in A.A. have very happy homes." This short sentence evokes everything from derisive snorts to happy nods of recognition whenever it is read aloud—a range of responses with which most married folks in any Twelve Step program will identify, depending on their time in recovery.

Here's the deal: You may think that your spouse will be so thrilled that you are finally, finally, finally taking the positive action of working a Twelve Step program that you'll be supported in countless terrific and uplifting ways. Your spouse will joyfully accompany you to open meetings and happily drive you to and from ones that are closed. You may think your spouse will be so filled with gratitude at your willingness to get better, so awed by your newfound spiritual commitments, that you'll be showered with praise for this awfully courageous and authentic thing you're doing. A dozen roses or a brand-new set of fleece seat covers will be delivered to you with delighted kisses when you complete your ninety days.

You should be so lucky.

In fact, some married folks are. What's much more likely is that your spouse or life partner will totally flip as you stop drinking, using, gambling, smoking, or overeating, as all the associated not-so-terrific behaviors that accompany active addiction start to flare up and then fade. Count on a lot of stumbling and fumbling for the first year or two. Possibly three or four. (Sorry, but it's a "program of honesty.") Don't be surprised if you're pelted with bursts of outright anger and hostility from your beloved, especially during your first ninety days. *After all, you changed both the music and the dance.*

If you got married while you were boozing, using, and whatever else, you cut a silent deal with your spouse wherein you got to play perpetrator/victim over and over again—usually switching roles according to no particular pattern or schedule. If you actually managed to marry someone who isn't an addict—a virtual impossibility because of the frequency with which like attract like—then cleaning up your act will be perceived as a direct threat to the balance of emotional power. Suddenly, the status of "suffering sober spouse" is rendered moot. The dynamics that invariably surround this revelation are not pretty. You might consider making the Serenity Prayer your new *mantra*.

If you married another active addict, you can bet (if you don't also have a gambling addiction, in which case focus on another idiom) that your recovery will be perceived as a major threat. Major. You just welshed on another deal wherein you both tacitly agreed to aid and abet each other's insanity. Suddenly your spouse is the sole surviving addict. The dynamics that surround this revelation can also become ugly. You may even have to temporarily leave if you can't get the active addict out of the home. (Talk to an attorney first so you don't unwittingly forfeit any property or support rights.)

Basically, things get real dicey when a married person gets into recovery. It is not at all unusual, and some might argue totally predictable, for marriages to dissolve as one spouse gets more and more sober. As the marriage changes, the one working a program of recovery usually starts asking, "What was I thinking?" The one still using usually asks, "What the hell is going on?"

*This is make or break time. Only the totally surrendered survive.* Ancillary "anon" programs (e.g., Al-Anon, Co-Anon, Gam-Anon, Nar-Anon) can be tremendously helpful. This might also be the point at which you and your spouse seek out professional support in the form of a psychotherapist.

So, should you be lining up your divorce attorney at Day 91? Nah. If you're following suggestions, you ain't making any major changes for a year, anyway.

Just don't use, do go to meetings, call your sponsor, reach out, work the Steps, and get involved in service. Get into the habit of invoking the slogans "Easy does it" and "Time takes time." There are plenty of people whose marriages were transformed from a living hell to almost paradise after everyone straightened up and out. If you're glumly married, find these people. Listen to their inspiring stories of hope, and pray that you won't be forced at some point to choose between your sobriety and your marriage.

## Are You Single?

Some would rightfully argue that anyone who starts this recovery business as a single person is enormously blessed.

> "Addicts don't have relationships; they take hostages."

So much so that it just might be enough to make you believe in a Higher Power, if you don't already.

Before you start feeling sorry for yourself because you're having this life-changing experience without a partner in tow, listen very carefully to what those who are already hitched share in the meetings. Now, aren't you grateful that you get to find out who *you* are before having to negotiate an intimate relationship with anyone else? No? Then go to a lot more meetings and listen more closely.

Being single gives you the time and space to learn how to live like a clean, sober, and abstinent person without having to negotiate the murky, turbulent waters of a relationship at the same time. During early recovery, you have the luxury of having crying jags, throwing temper tantrums, and listening to really annoying music over and over and over again without anyone around to observe this lunacy. As you acquire more time, you have the privilege of spending hours on the phone with program pals and traipsing off to commitments in small migratory herds without any special someone feeling excluded, abandoned, or flat-out jealous.

When you are ready for an intimate relationship, you—unlike your married counterparts—will do it as a (relatively) sober person. And if you wait long enough before pairing off, you may even manage to choose an appropriate partner for the first time in your life.

And what constitutes waiting "long enough"? The

very strong suggestion that anyone not already in a relationship really ought to stay that way for at least an entire year is well worth following. Most people are in a total fog their first year of recovery. Conventional program wisdom has it that it takes at least five years to get one's "brains out of hock." Do you have to wait *that* long? Nope. But it is kind of interesting to note that by the time you're "allowed" to date you may be up to realizing how unqualified you are to do so. Of course, anyone in recovery from love and/or sex addiction will need to be extra-vigilant and rigorously honest about the motivation for exploring any intimate relationship. (If it's any consolation, every great religious tradition—both Western and Eastern—views voluntary celibacy as a powerful spiritual practice.)

Having said all this, Twelve Step meetings and activities offer singles abundant opportunities to thoroughly check out potential partners well in advance. People attend meetings in various stages of emotional and physical dishabille, revealing more about themselves over time than they ever could on a series of dates. Where else could you so closely observe someone's ability to manage a wide range of life situations over a period of years?

☛ As a general rule, share feelings with the group and specifics with your sponsor. Your sponsor presumably has the time, energy, and interest to hear a play-by-play description of what may be threatening your sobriety and serenity. Saying, for example, "My job is being downsized, and I'm feeling angry and scared" provides enough information for groups members to start sharing their "experience, strength, and hope."

Hey, don't worry about missing any unsolicited feedback. After the meeting, you'll be surrounded by a gaggle of people who are only too willing to listen to whatever gory details you feel compelled to spill—in exchange for telling you how to handle your "crisis du jour."

## What about Therapy?

Well, what about it? For every person who has started a program of recovery at the suggestion of a savvy therapist, there are a dozen addicts still out there because they've boondoggled their helping professionals into believing that drinking, using, or compulsively doing wasn't an issue. Which is to say, going to a therapist and getting therapeutic help ain't necessarily the same thing.

Nevertheless, there are some problems that will not and cannot be addressed (let alone "fixed") by your sponsor or well-meaning, but untrained, friends.

Go to therapy, if

- after you've stopped using and have worked the Steps for a while, a horrifying abundance of awful memories ooze up to the surface from the muck of your subconscious
- everyone says you're walking your talk, but you still feel like total crap
- you acquire and fire (or are fired by) sponsors in two- to four-month cycles, or change your friendship network almost as often
- you use Twelve Step meetings as an economical and convenient form of group therapy

For now, skip therapy and focus on total Twelve Step immersion if

- you've already done heavy therapeutic time in any number of modalities and it never stopped you from using
- deep down inside (or even closer to the surface) you hope your therapist will recommend you take drugs

- you happen to be a helping professional and think one more consultation about your DSM-IV category will make a difference in your addictive behavior

## Choosing a Therapist

Let's say you really do need therapy and are finally ready to do the hard work of discovering, confronting, and healing the psyche. If you're committed to recovery, you'll have to find a therapist who embraces a certain set of concepts about addiction. As a general rule, avoid any practitioner who has yet to realize that addiction is a complex phenomenon involving body, mind, and spirit.

Shop for someone who

- not only understands family systems, but who more specifically understands the funky, convoluted dynamics of families riddled with addiction
- is trained in a practical, action-oriented modality such as cognitive therapy, which helps untangle twisted patterns of negative self-talk (as opposed to a more psychoanalytic approach where you'll spend endless hours spelunking the past)
- has, in addition to other formal training, legitimate, well-regarded certification in addictions counseling
- is practically grounded in the reality of the havoc that is wreaked by addiction but also has faith
- will refer you to a psychiatrist for evaluation if you or family members have a history of illnesses involving brain biochemistry disorders which, if left medically untreated, will result in psychosis

Being hospitalized, bedridden, or otherwise housebound can be painful and depressing for "civilians." For those in

"When you're home by yourself, you're behind enemy lines."

recovery, such a level of isolation can be positively dangerous. This would be a good time to practice asking for what you need, including

- meetings held in your hospital room or at your home
- prepared meals, library books, or brain candy from the video store
- rides to meetings, doctors, physical therapy, or even somewhere fun

☞ Communication is at the heart of any successful relationship both in and out of the program, and honesty is the proverbial bedrock of Twelve Step recovery work. For addicts who have evaded the truth about themselves and/or lied about it to others, speaking authentically, openly, and directly about *anything* can be quite a shock to the system. *You will undoubtedly need to practice telling the truth.* To practice honest communication try the following exercises:

- Stop yourself from telling any more of those "little white lies" that habitually tumble out of your mouth for no darn good reason, except that it always *seems* easier than telling the truth. For example, admit you spaced out and forgot to check the time instead of fabricating a horrendous traffic jam. Start doing this and watch your relationships begin to improve.
- Tell "on yourself" in meetings or to program pals when you catch yourself cheating, skidding around the truth, or outright lying. Communicating the truth after the fact is better than never doing so at all. Also, doing so may help you discern patterns in your less-than-authentic communications. For example, do you shamelessly embellish when you're feeling fabulous? How about when you're feeling little? Do you understate problems when

you're afraid of what others might think about your cop-ing abilities? Inviting (safe) others to help you identify patterns is another way to build authentic relationships.
- Learn and, most important, use these handy relation-ship-building phrases:
  - I need help.
  - I don't know.
  - I feel scared.
  - Thank you.

☞ People tend to respond better when requests are clear, specific, and have obvious limits. Keeping this in mind will greatly improve your chances of success in building reliable and mutually satisfactory relationships.

Practically speaking, this means asking, "Will you be able to give me a ride to the Thursday meeting this week?" when that's exactly what you need. This is ever so much more effec-tive than wistfully wondering out loud, "Can you give me a ride sometime?"

☞ Before getting into a program of recovery, you probably handled conflict by going stone-cold silent, muttering under your breath, being belligerent, or getting into shouting matches with perceived opponents.

Hanging out with others in recovery will provide plenty of opportunities to hear divergent opinions. Instead of immediately seeking to establish *your truth*, practice (nicely) asking others to help you understand their point of view.

☞ As long as you're learning how to speak honestly and au-thentically, you may as well tackle the entire communications repertoire and learn how to listen as well. Why? Active addicts don't listen well. They are either too busy talking over, around, or through others; distracted by dreaming and scheming; or simply out of it.

Listening involves a tad more than not speaking, although keeping one's mouth shut is certainly a necessary first step. *Practice makes for progress, if not perfection.* When someone is speaking and you're supposed to be listening, try the following techniques:

> "Say what you mean, mean what you say, but don't say it mean."

- Make and maintain eye contact—gently. No weird glazed-over staring or glaring.
- Lean slightly toward that person without looming, hovering, or otherwise violating personal space.
- Nod sympathetically at the moments you will know are appropriate because you truly will be listening.
- Remain silent until the other person has completely finished his or her soliloquy. No jumping right in at the slightest pause for breath.

☞ There's a difference between reaching out and butting in. Focusing on someone else's strange behavior is bound to distract you from working your own program of recovery. Whenever you find yourself obsessing about what other people are doing or saying, stop and ask yourself whether the situation

- has anything directly to do with you
- is something you can do anything about

☞ Friendships, let alone intimate relationships, can be difficult for people in general. They're almost unfathomable for those who spent their formative social years under the influence of alcohol or other drugs. They are likewise mysterious and sometimes scary for anyone who has used substances, food, or activities like gambling as a social stimulant and lubricant. Here are some safe ways to develop friendships in recovery:

> **"What other people think about you is none of your business."**

• Make Twelve Step fellowship activities the foundation of your social life, until you get a life.

• Attend social events—dinners out, movies, concerts, parties—in small groups of people who are also working a program of recovery.

• Limit social engagements to short, manageable chunks of time (e.g., yet another cup of coffee after the meeting, a half-hour walk around a nature preserve).

• Offer or get rides to meetings with the same people on a regular basis.

• Volunteer to set up before or clean up after meetings.

## Sex

Your sex life started out . . . well, you're not exactly sure because you were loaded at the time and so was your partner. Come to think of it, you can't remember engaging in any kind of sexual intimacy without "getting in the mood" before and lighting the proverbial cigarette, chowing down, or totally passing out immediately thereafter.

Maybe you actually did engage in something you considered "lovemaking" once or twice, but over the years those memories have been obliterated by feelings of resentment, guilt, or disgust. While active in your addiction, you did any number of things you'd much rather forget: You forced your partner to engage in activities that he or she didn't like, or you tried things that you would never agree to in recovery. You thought nothing of supplementing marital relations with a little adulterous nooky. Orgasm? Ejaculation? Nada. Substances had so wrecked your nervous system that you couldn't follow through once you got started.

If just reading this list brings up the hot flush of shame, take a deep breath, relax, and allow yourself to feel flushed with gratitude instead. In recovery, you have a chance to make sexual intimacy feel right, good, and whole. Time, clean living, healthy nutrition, and better sleep will heal the physiological damage. Time and rigorous Step work, augmented perhaps by some psychological counseling, will take care of the emotional and spiritual wreckage. This healing will take some time because, after all, "Time takes time." Meanwhile, be gentle with yourself and others.

If you're sexually active, consider taking a break from sex until you clear out whatever has heretofore blocked the path to true sober intimacy. Working Steps Four through Nine will help you acknowledge the impact of old hurts, disappointments, and resentments. Going on a "sex fast" will also help you distinguish sexual activity from intimacy, romance from reality, and manipulation from affection. At the very least, take a break from sexual activity until you educate yourself about necessity for and practicalities of practicing "safe" sex. You were probably too busy using and abusing to fully comprehend the killer nature of today's sexually transmitted diseases.

☛ Don't know what to ask for, let alone how to receive anything? For a day, week, or month, ask for help doing whatever you automatically think you can, or should be able to, do all by yourself:

- figuring out how to install computer software
- repainting the kitchen
- finding a medical specialist

- consulting with an attorney
- changing hair stylists
- visiting your mother

## Supermarket Safari

What's it like to go food shopping in recovery? For some who cannot imagine entering a food emporium without being blasted, blitzed, smashed, stoned, trippy, wasted, zoned, or zonked, it can be pretty freaky. Your days and nights of eating peanut butter out of a jar with your fingers and washing it down with nothing remotely healthy *must* come to an end!

Eating well is essential to continued recovery and buying the proper food is an important first step. You just might need to put food shopping on your list of things to get help learning. Please don't let shyness or shame get in the way. If you have no idea how to stock a cupboard or refrigerator, you're not alone. Many a sponsor has given guided tours of supermarkets to dazed newcomers who think the four major food groups are salty, crunchy, caffeine, and chocolate.

## Anon and On and On

At the dawn of Twelve Step time, Bill Wilson's long-suffering wife, Lois, and other female captives dutifully attended meetings with their husbands. (Come to think of it, this is probably how the tradition of continuous coffee was established. After all, they had to do *something* to stay awake during meetings that lasted much longer than a measly little hour.)

As the fellowship of Alcoholics Anonymous developed

and grew, the ladies formed their own auxiliary. Nowadays, "anon" groups are open to everyone related to, or involved with, anyone either active in addiction or pursuing recovery. Numerous anon groups exist to complement the primary recovery programs for every conceivable addiction.

People who attend these groups, which provide a safe place to share tales of woe, have sometimes been uncharitably referred to as a "bunch of whiners" by those in primary programs of recovery. Still, these ancillary groups are probably responsible for staving off a fair number of spousal homicides and other forms of mayhem within families and friendship networks. They help willing attendees recover from the primary affliction of those involved with an addict—incredibly lousy personal boundaries and the compulsive need to fix everyone *else* (aka codependency).

And, if an anon group doesn't help loosen the suction on your emotional tentacles, there's an entire Twelve Step program called Co-Dependents Anonymous (CoDA) which focuses on the business of minding one's own business.

Don't be surprised if, after a while, your sponsor strongly suggests you attend one of these groups yourself. Why? Because if you stick with the program long enough, most, if not all, of your nearest and dearest friends will be in recovery, and you'll need to attend an anon group to learn how to get along with *them!*

The body-mind connection is both powerful and instructive. Recognizing the connection between what you think and how you feel—both physically and emotionally—will help you learn how to establish healthy boundaries.

Physical indicators such as headaches, nausea, sudden exhaustion, cold sweats, and breaking out in big pink splotchy patches are worth noting. So are emotional reactions such as anxiety, annoyance, embarrassment, and anger.

Sometimes a physical symptom may be a manifestation of an emotional reaction (e.g., migraine headaches that can be traced back to unexpressed anger). It doesn't matter which you zoom in on first— the physical or emotional (i.e., the migraine or the anger). Use either and preferably both forms of data to just say "no" to certain people, places, and situations.

> "There are no victims, only volunteers."

☞ Learn how to identify and sort out feelings by describing in writing what triggered the emotion, where you felt it in your body, and what the feeling felt like. Recording as much data as possible about what is giving rise to the feeling will help you better sort the "good" triggers from the "bad." Sometimes it all feels the same!

If, for example, you received a certified letter and felt your stomach flip with what felt like nausea, you could be feeling either anxiety or excitement, depending on the return address. Certified letter from the Internal Revenue Service? Anxiety. Certified letter from the Publishers Clearinghouse? Excitement.

Get into the habit of writing this stuff out, and eventually you'll be able to distinguish sadness from depression, fear from anger, this from that.

☞ You can expect to feel a bit odd—okay, downright cuckoo— as your anniversary date draws nigh. It is extremely common, even predictable, for people to be flooded with memories of hitting bottom for weeks (or sometimes months) before celebrating the important milestones of recovery. Talking about such feelings will help diffuse them.

☞ Procure one of those posters with the ubiquitous (and annoying) yellow happy face expressing a wide range of feelings. Use this goofy (and annoying) visual aid to learn how to discern the nuances of emotions.

## Feelings, oh-oh-oh Feelings

As you become more active in a Twelve Step program, you'll notice that there are people who genuinely seem interested in your well-being. They will ask how you are doing, and in response you'll probably mutter "fine" or "okay." As the fog clears, you may be moved to answer "I don't know" or "haven't a clue" when the question gets put to you. This is good. It means you're becoming more honest with yourself which is definitely a prerequisite for becoming more honest with others.

Eventually, you'll be able to make greater distinctions among feelings. Foreign-sounding words like "happy," "sad," or "angry" will pop out of your mouth. You may even admit to feeling "fearful." But wait, there's more!

Amazingly, these core feelings will expand and deepen. As you reach out, you will discover a host of even more subtle emotions, either because you will personally feel them or because some sort of cosmic lightbulb goes off in your psyche when others share about feeling them.

*Here are some of the emotions that await you in recovery.* Try not to get too hung up on evaluating or judging these feeling states. Some are delightful. Some stink. None of them are "real," even though they may be triggered by very real events. Keep this slogan in mind: "Feelings are not facts." Note: The words on the following list are *alphabetized,* so don't wrack your brain trying to figure out if they've been listed in the right order!

**HAPPY**
Amused
Blissful
Confident
Contented
Delighted
Eager
Ecstatic
Enthusiastic
Excited
Glad
Joyous
Mellow
Optimistic
Pleased
Relieved
Satisfied
Serene
Thrilled
Triumphant

**SAD**
Apathetic
Bored
Disappointed
Disinterested
Exhausted
Helpless
Hurt
Indifferent
Lonely
Miserable
Pained

Passive
Regretful
Tired
Withdrawn

**FEARFUL**
Anxious
Apprehensive
Ashamed
Bashful
Cautious
Concerned
Confused
Embarrassed
Frantic
Frightened
Greedy
Guilty
Horrified
Hysterical
Insecure
Jealous
Nervous
Overwhelmed
Perplexed
Puzzled
Scared
Sheepish
Shy
Skeptical
Suspicious
Terrified
Threatened

Timid
Uncertain
Vulnerable
Worried

**ANGRY**
Aggressive
Annoyed
Cold
Contemptuos
Cranky
Depressed
Disgusted
Enraged
Exasperated
Frustrated
Horrified
Hostile
Infuriated
Negative
Peeved
Resentful
Shocked
Sulky
Sullen

**LOVING**
Grateful
Hopeful
Kindly
Sympathetic
Tender
Thoughtful

# 4

## Working the Steps

Some people in recovery really truly believe that simply not using and faithfully attending meetings is enough to keep them clean, sober, and abstinent. It isn't. At the heart of any Twelve Step program is . . . the Twelve Steps! If you want continued recovery, you'll need to "work" them.

Do you have to? Nope. Other than the essential First Step, which requires a full admission of powerlessness over whatever substance or behavior is doing you in, the rest of the Steps are considered "suggestions." Nevertheless, they're darned good ones and have a proven track record for helping even the most hopeless of cases. The success of Twelve Step recovery programs is due to participants making substantial (and substantive) changes in attitude and behavior.

So, what's this "work" business about?

Each Step requires you to take an unflinching look at the sources and patterns of your addiction. Each Step involves taking some kind of action to change from the person you were while active to the person you can become in recovery. Stop a nanosecond to think about what it has ever taken to jolt you into a new way of being, and you'll understand why this Twelve Step process is considered work.

Get ready to do a lot of honest thinking, writing, and speaking. These activities can come as quite a shock if you've spent most of your life in "fire, aim, ready" mode and fast-talking around situations. Plan to slow way down in order to pay closer attention to your stuff. While you're at it, plan to stock up on stationery supplies. You'll be spending a fair amount of time making lists, keeping a journal, and writing letters that you may or may not actually send. Don't worry if writing isn't your thing. You won't be submitting any of it to judges for the National Book Award. What you will be doing is sharing your "progress not perfection" with the sponsor you now have because you took chapter 4 to heart!

Buckle up for a radical journey through Self. You will build a foundation of willingness and belief by working Steps One and Two. Steps Three through Nine will require decisions and actions that would never have occurred to you in your pre-recovery daze. What happens next is really freaky. The amazing results you get from making sober decisions and taking sober actions will, by working Steps Ten through Twelve, lead you to a life of faith. And if the prospect of *that* makes you anxious about becoming a religious fanatic, relax. By the time this transformation occurs, you'll be very clear about the key differences between spirituality and religion.

Here's another preview: Somewhere along the way you're going to realize that you've stumbled into one of the greatest "bait and switch" schemes of all time. You entered a Twelve Step program to handle a slight drinking, drugging, gambling, overeating, promiscuity, smoking, or shopping problem. Well, that's the *least* of what's going to happen. Plan on having your entire life changed. Fortunately, none of this happens overnight. None of this happens one moment before it's supposed to happen. Use the tips in this chapter to work the Twelve Steps one day at a time and try not to worry about a future, albeit a wonderful one, that isn't here yet.

## CHAPTER TIPS

☞ Try not to get too distracted by the archaic language that permeates much of the older "official" Twelve Step literature. If you spend time rewriting it in your head, you'll miss whatever else is going on during meetings—or in your guts. Instead, pretend you're reading a period-piece novel or a historical document. Allow yourself to be charmed by old-fashioned idioms and references to yesteryear. Expand your vocabulary by looking up words you don't readily recognize or understand.

☞ Buy your very own copies of program literature and underline passages that have special meaning for you. Scribble notes in the margins, dating them and/or using a variety of colors to represent different passes through the same material. Invest in a new copy when the text is so marked up that you can barely read it.

Remember: Addiction is a family disease, so be sure to save your retired literature. It's destined to become a family heirloom.

☞ Having trouble understanding the Steps?
- Dedicate a period of time—a month, ninety days, a year—to saturating yourself with meetings focused specifically on reading and discussing the Steps. No Step meetings in your area? Help start one.

- Learn the Steps according to key action words:
  1.........Admit
  2.........Believe
  3.........Decide
  4.........Search
  5.........Confess
  6.........Ready

7.........Ask
8.........Willing
9.........Amend
10........Continue
11........Sought
12........Carry

• Learn the Steps according to key concepts:
1.........Powerlessness
2.........Came to Believe
3.........Turning It Over
4.........Moral Inventory
5.........Admit Wrongs
6.........Entirely Ready
7.........Humbly Asked
8.........Willingness
9.........Direct Amends
10........Promptly Admitted
11........Conscious Contact
12........Practicing Principles

• Or learn the short version:
1.........Acceptance
2.........Faith
3.........Surrender and Trust
4.........Honesty
5.........Courage
6.........Willingness
7.........Humility
8.........Forgiveness
9.........Freedom
10.......Perseverance
11.......Patience
12.......Charity and Love

- Write them out on sticky notes that you post in places where you cannot help but see them, such as the bathroom mirror, refrigerator door, or remote control for the television.
- Just show up, listen carefully, and trust the process.

☞ Work the Steps in the order they were written, looping back to redo the foundational first three as often as necessary to keep your focus on recovery.

> "Don't worry if you don't get it right away. It will eventually get you."

☞ Never mind trying to complete one Step per week, month, or year. You'll be ready to move on to the next one when the following things occur:

- You can recall and recite the Step you've been working without inadvertently leaving out key words or phrases such as "powerless," "searching and fearless," "admitted," "entirely ready," or "God."
- The Step you're working suddenly makes perfect sense. It feels like something you've always known, part of your cell structure.
- Your sponsor suggests that you do.

## Simply Put: Step One

*We admitted we were powerless over [fill in the blank]— that our lives had become unmanageable.*

You've become a slave to whatever you're incessantly using or doing. Ease up on the value judgments and don't squander precious energy debating whether your family, biology, or demonic forces are at fault. For now, all you have to do is admit that your life is an uncontrollable mess because what you thought you were controlling is instead controlling you. Big time.

☞ Make a list of everything from minor skirmishes to major screwups in your life. Carefully review each and every strange-but-true event and write about it, noting

- whether you had engaged in your addictive activity of choice within thirty-six hours before what law enforcement officials would politely call "the incident."
- the status of your addiction at the time. Were you occasionally, casually indulging? Carefully controlling? If so, how? White-knuckling it? Totally out of control? Gee whiz, just can't remember?

Don't skimp on the details! Write paragraphs if need be to help you see the true causal connection between your addiction and getting in trouble. Also notice when and how your addiction escalated or, as they say, "progressed."

## Coincidence or Correlation?

For your own enlightenment and perhaps a bizarre bit of fun, match the activities in column A with as many column B consequences that apply.

| Column A | Column B |
|---|---|
| *While You Were . . .* | *This Happened "to" You . . .* |
| Drinking | Fist fights |
| Smoking cigarettes | Employment termination |
| Snorting cocaine | Switched jobs a lot |
| Betting | Dropped out of school |
| Smoking crack | Attempted suicide |
| Binge/purge eating | Stopped by police |
| Shooting heroin | Sued for divorce |

| | |
|---|---|
| Getting laid a lot | Major health problems |
| Haunting casinos | Legal skirmishes |
| Smoking dope | Jail time |
| Overloading credit cards | Gave up on God |
| Sniffing glue | Disowned by parents |
| Popping pills | Minor health problems |
| Running numbers | Vomited blood |
| Tripping your brains out | Lost housing |
| | Car repossessed |
| | Thrown out of school |
| | Borrowed money |
| | License(s) revoked |
| | Lost child custody |
| | Denied insurance coverage |
| | Bankruptcy |

☛ Do a little personal archaeology to get a better sense of your life's unmanageability. For the period of time you were active in your addiction, dig up and then examine copies of your

- personnel files from wherever you worked
- military records, especially if you served overseas
- police reports and legal actions
- hospital records and doctor's bills
- credit-card statements and check registers
- diary of whacked-out diatribes about who did you wrong and how life stinks

Note: It's extremely useful and revealing to do this at different points in your recovery. What you blew off as "no big deal" in your first year may become horrifyingly pertinent by the time you make it to year three.

☛ Have no idea how your life was unmanageable? It's never too late to do an intervention on yourself. After quietly announcing that you're finally doing some soul-searching, request that significant others tell you honestly, directly, and as kindly as possible how they've perceived your attitude, emotions, and behaviors over the years.

Do not sabotage this exercise by asking unindicted coconspirators to share their views. Instead, dare to ask your beleaguered spouse or intimate partner, put-upon work colleagues, disgusted siblings, or mortified kids to

- give concrete examples of how your addiction has affected family, social, and work activities
- describe in detail any less-than-lovely behaviors they perceive as being connected to your addiction
- remind you about accidents and dangerous situations resulting from your active addiction
- recall any financial difficulties that seemed to be linked to your addiction

Note: Don't be at all surprised if your respondents get a little cranky as they reminisce about your career as an addict. Remember your goal: to collect useful data. Make every effort to control the human knee-jerk impulse to self-justify.

## The Victory of Defeat

Wait. Isn't it supposed to be the *agony* of defeat? Only according to sports commentators. On the playing field of life, the reverse is true: There can be no complete victory without complete defeat.

This call to willingly surrender everything, or eventually lose it in exchange for true freedom, is one of those pesky, metaphysical, can't-wrap-the-brain-around-it truisms that pervade the world's great religious traditions.

In Psalm 71, the psalmist sings, "Though you have made me see troubles, many and bitter, you will restore my life again; from the depths of the earth you will again bring me up." In the Brihad-Aranyaka Upanishad, the yogi prays: "From the unreal lead me to the real! From darkness lead me to light! From death lead me to immortality!" The prayer attributed to Saint Francis of Assisi, much loved and oft recited by Twelve Step devotees, ends by noting that "it is in dying that we are born to eternal life."

The victory of defeat.

This experience of being razed before being raised seems to be especially true of addicts for whom bottoming-out provides the necessary (but decidedly insufficient) impetus to get it together. For most, bottoming-out is a process rather than an event. Only a lucky few only trip and fall once. Everyone else cycles through physical, emotional, financial, and spiritual catastrophes before becoming desperate enough to take the first wobbly steps toward recovery with its promise of liberation.

## Simply Put: Step Two

*Came to believe that a Power greater than ourselves could restore us to sanity.*

Maybe *you're* not technically nuts, but your behaviors sure are. At some point, it's going to dawn on you that all your feeble human attempts to change ain't worth squat. Something greater than you could indeed save you from yourself, but only if you believe it could. (Relax. No one is commanding you to believe in God.)

☞ To help grasp the concept of a power greater than yourself, spend some time where you can palpably feel your own insignificance:

- Visit an awe-inspiring natural wonder like the Grand Canyon, Niagara Falls, or better yet, a mountain range unsullied by hordes of tourists.
- Stand in a field filled with fireflies on a summer night and let yourself be serenaded by crickets.
- Gaze at a huge glowing orange harvest moon on an autumn evening.
- Find an empty cathedral complete with flying buttresses, gorgeous stained glass windows, and a nave the length of a football field; then sit quietly in one of the rear pews for a while.
- Spend at least twelve hours in the emergency room of an urban hospital on a Saturday night, preferably on a holiday weekend.
- Walk a leashed dog where there are an abundance of squirrels.

> "Insanity is continuing to do the same thing over and over, while expecting different results."

☞ Keep a written record of every amazing, unbelievable thing that seems to have happened by coincidence, as a result of circumstance, and without you doing anything since you started working your program of recovery.

☞ If the word "God" gives you the heebie jeebies, don't use it. Focus instead on believing that something or someone greater, more powerful, and certainly more knowledgeable than you can provide help:

- an outpatient program at the rehab
- the Twelve Step recovery fellowship at large
- an addictions counselor or therapist
- a sponsor
- your cat

☞ Conduct a mini-survey of those who claim to have a spiritual Higher Power. Ask these folks if they came into recovery believing in a Higher Power, when and why their attitude changed, and how having a supernatural source of help makes a difference in their recovery. Simply sip your coffee and listen to what they have to say.

## Simply Put: Step Three

*Made a decision to turn our will and our lives over to the care of God* as we understood Him.

You're finally convinced that you've bungled the business of living. You now take action by deciding to turn everything over to a Higher Power, one that you alone get to define and may or may not call "God."

☞ If, at this point, you are still indulging in your primary addiction, you really ought to seriously consider stopping because your addiction continues to be your Higher Power. Return to the first two Steps for a longer visit.

> "All you need to know about God is that you're not God."

☞ Remember who or what you designated as your Higher Power while working Step Two? Now it's time to ask for and allow yourself to accept help from

- an outpatient program at the rehab
- the Twelve Step recovery fellowship at large
- an addictions counselor or therapist
- a sponsor
- your cat

☞ If the God of your understanding isn't loving, compassionate, and forgiving, you'll need to concoct one that is. While you're at it, make sure the God of your understanding has a terrific sense of humor.

☞ To become more aware of how and why you make the decisions you make, slow your decision-making process way down. Learn and use these handy phrases at work, at home, and at play:

- Let me get back to you on that.
- I need time to think this one through.
- I'm not sure if this is right for me.
- Can you give me a little more information?
- When do you need an answer?

☞ Before making decisions of any magnitude that might be a manifestation of your incredible need to get whatever you want when you want it, think your willfulness through by asking yourself these questions:

- Is this going to support or undermine my recovery?
- What would my sponsor suggest I do? (You can also call to find out!)
- What are my motives for doing this? Am I being defiant? Playing brinkmanship? Retaliating? Taking the easy way out? Trying to look better, nicer, more generous, or more humble than I really am?
- How does doing what I want to do when I want to do it affect my family, friends, and co-workers?
- If I saw other people in recovery making the decision I'm about to make, would I be accusing them of "self-will run riot"?

☞ There are darn few decisions that can't be put on hold until you make at least three phone calls and wait at least twenty-four hours. Since addicts are famous for diving into things without doing a lot of research or considering the consequences, regard the adrenaline rush of urgency as a strong signal to s-l-o-w d-o-w-n.

## Stomaching the Slogans

Unless you've come into the program extraordinarily fond of cheerful refrigerator magnets, use happy faces to punctuate your sentences, and think the word "gay" always refers to sprightly gingham tablecloths, you will undoubtedly gag when you first hear the beloved slogans. Then, as with everything else in a Twelve Step program of recovery, they will not only start making sense but also become a source of illuminating comfort.

Not only will you stop wanting to smack the next person who recites one, but you will also hear them tumble gracefully from your own mouth. Someday you will find yourself smiling with fraternal recognition as the slogans whiz by in traffic. Don't be surprised if you eventually end up sticking one of those glittery slogan stickers on the bumper of your own car.

The ultimate appeal of the slogans that emerged out of the literature of Alcoholics Anonymous lies in their simplicity—and brevity. The slogans offer a quick, handy, and memorable way to keep mindful of program principles.

Plan on hearing—and hopefully stomaching—the following slogans, especially during your first few years of recovery. Here's what they mean:

**One day at a time.**
Translation: Don't fret about the rest of your life; just stay clean, sober, and abstinent for today.

**First things first.**
Translation: Make your recovery your top priority, and everything else will fall into place.

**Stick with the winners.**
Translation: Notice whose program seems to be working and do what they did.

**Easy does it.**
Translation: Slow down and relax. Don't take on more than you can handle.

**Progress not perfection.**
Translation: Any effort to change, no matter how seemingly minor, counts.

Instead of waiting to fully experience the consequences of your decisions, boldly experiment with thinking through the predictable sequence of events. First, remember a similar situation. Okay, what did you decide to do? What action did you actually take? With what results? Does the action you're now contemplating bear *any* resemblance to what you've done before? Now, connect those dots. Still want to do it the old way?

You can do this exercise while sitting on your sofa and staring into middle distance, by talking it through with your sponsor, or by writing it out.

By the way, if you can't remember the Twelve Step definition of "insanity," anyone in recovery will be more than happy to recite it to you.

Two ways of dealing with the spiritual supernatural God-stuff component of the Third Step:

1. Plunge ahead on pure faith, turning your life and your will over to God as you understand God.
2. Wait until you feel ready (i.e., more miserable).

☞ Use "God" as an acronym. If you're in Alcoholics Anonymous, it can mean "Group of Drunks." Or you can think of it as "Good Orderly Direction." Dog spelled backwards. Whatever gets you past the God thing and into taking positive forward action in recovery.

> **"Fear is the absence of faith."**

☞ Notice whether the decisions you make seem to have an annoying way of not working out or becoming awfully convoluted. Adopt the rules of baseball and go back to the bench after three strikes. While benched, consider the possibility that complications might indicate that what you want opposes the will of God . . . the Universe . . . the Divine Order of Things . . . and so on.

## Simply Put: Step Four

*Made a searching and fearless moral inventory of ourselves.*

Now you're ready to thoroughly catalog pre-recovery exploits in order to discover what's lurking beneath that oh-so-draining addiction.

☞ When to do the Fourth Step?
- You've taken the first three Steps and are totally willing to retake them as often as necessary to stay with the process of recovery.
- You're obsessed with the past, suffused with pain and shame over things done and not done, said and unsaid.
- You've thrown so many pity parties that no one other than you attends anymore.
- Your sponsor shifts out of Suggestion Mode and flat-out tells you to.
- It's long overdue.

☞ Offset the potentially nerve-wracking Fourth Step experience of fearless self-examination and scrupulous honesty by creating as much safety and comfort for yourself as possible in a clean, sober, and abstinent way. Depending on your program of recovery, you'll need to take this Step without draining buckets of beer, snorting anything, watching the home-shopping networks, or devouring a cheesecake (or three) during the process. Aim for a subtle jostling, as opposed to a violent triggering, of memory by gently appealing to the senses. In addition to the self-soothing tips in chapter 1, try the following techniques:

> **"We're only as sick as our secrets."**

- Put on music that's unobtrusive enough to support your concentration, such as something instrumental from the baroque era (end of sixteenth century to early eighteenth century). You already have enough drama going on in your head, so avoid listening to songs with intense lyrics. If you simply must have company, listen to a Gregorian chant, which is slow, repetitive, and usually in liturgical Latin.

- Light incense and candles unless doing so was an integral part of your getting-wasted protocol, in which case skip it.

- Make sure Spot or Fluffy is curled up on your lap, unless, of course, your beloved pet produces buckets of drool, sheds uncontrollably, has fleas, or weighs over twenty pounds.

- If it's cold outside, put on your favorite jammies or sweat suit; then wrap yourself up in a cozy blanket. If it's balmy, go to a park and lean up against a sturdy tree. If it's hot and you have access to one, go sit on the beach.

- Find quiet safe space in the public library or a pew at a house of worship.

☛ Even if you type as quickly as thoughts bubble up in your brain, consider writing out your Fourth Step inventory by hand instead of banging it out on a computer keyboard. Longhand will slow you down, giving you time to contemplate what you're committing to paper.

☛ Enhance the tactile experience of writing out your Fourth Step inventory by choosing a soft pencil or a flowing ink pen that feels good in your hand. Enhance the visual experience by choosing paper that's pleasing to your eye.

## Making a List, Checking It Twice, Gonna Find Out . . .

The Fourth Step inventory is a process rife with paradox. The actual writing may make filling out your income tax returns look like no big deal. And yet, the enormous sense of relief and freedom that many people feel after completing this task makes the hassle well worth it. Try to keep this in mind as you slog through everything you've been repressing and suppressing during years of addictive behavior.

The Fourth Step is the first of seven action-oriented Steps. In taking the Fourth Step you will, in fact, be taking several actions, some more challenging than others. If you've truly done the first three Steps, you've already tried—and hopefully experienced the rewards of—honesty. Now you're going to dive deeper into the truth by being "searching and fearless." You've already taken the action of admitting you were powerless. Now, you're going to admit specifics. Finally, you're going to take the action of getting all this junk out of your head and onto paper. This sometimes comes as a great shock to those who have somehow managed to avoid writing anything up to this point.

There is no shortage of pamphlets, workbooks, and guides to writing a Fourth Step inventory. The most comprehensive and allegedly simple approach can be found in the "Big Book" of Alcoholics Anonymous on pages 64–65, although you'd never know it because the directions are fairly convoluted. Basically, it asks you to look at resentments, fears, and persons harmed by your antics; then catalog the causes of each resentment, source of each fear, and what you did that was harmful. Next, you're asked to identify what part of Self was so threatened that you behaved the way you did. Finally, you're asked to name—exactly—the "nature" of your actions and reactions. In other words, you are asked to own up—in writing—to being selfish, dishonest, scared, manipulative, self-absorbed, and so on.

Does this seem daunting, depressing, and painful? Listen to those who've completed Fourth Step inventories, and they'll tell you it was *nothing* compared to the pain of addiction.

What? Just reading this has you glazing over? Okay. Forget about wading through a zillion guides. Go find something to write with, something to write on, and start writing out lists of everyone you resent, fear, and have hurt. Next, write about why, noting your role in the matter. Be specific: If you didn't pay bills on time, note that was because you blew bucks at the racetrack. If you missed your kid's school play, note that you were loaded at the time. If you were a no-show at a family funeral, note that you made drugging a priority instead.

That's it, for now.

You'll have plenty of time to find and analyze patterns of behavior during your Fifth Step.

☞ Give yourself a realistic time frame within which to complete your Fourth Step inventory. Figure that if you knock it off in three hours, you're probably not being searching enough. If you drag it out over a year, you're probably not being fearless. By all means account for the time sucked up by other responsibilities, but do not use a busy schedule as an excuse to either skip or drag your way through the Fourth Step inventory.

☞ Before picking up your pen or booting up the computer (because you *have* to type), ask the God of your understanding for the willingness, guidance, and courage to complete this important process of self-examination.

☞ You'll be doing more than one Fourth Step inventory during the lifetime of your recovery, so don't worry about the length of the first one you do. Rest assured that more gruesome details will come to mind as you become more clean, sober, and abstinent. Yippee!

## Simply Put: Step Five

*Admitted to God, to ourselves, and to another human being the exact nature of our wrongs.*

You're going to tell the truth about yourself to God—even if you believe God already knows. You're going to tell the truth about yourself to yourself—even though you're the one who wrote the blankety-blank Fourth Step. You're going to tell the truth about yourself to another human being—even when you'd much rather confess all into Fido's floppy ears.

☞ Assume in advance that God forgives you. Know in advance that forgiving yourself will come in time. Remember in advance that it's not up to another human being to judge you.

☞ Schedule your Fifth Step within a few days of completing your Fourth Step so you don't have to walk around too long with a freshly opened wound.

Think of the Fourth and Fifth Steps combined as a healing process; allowing weeks or months to drag by in between lancing a wound and letting it drain not only impedes healing, but may lead to reinfection.

☞ If you're Jewish, you can deepen the cleansing experience of working your Fifth Step by scheduling it between Rosh Hashanah (New Year) and Yom Kippur (Day of Atonement). You can add even more symbolic meaning to the event by starting to write your Fourth Step inventory during Passover, the holiday that celebrates victory from bondage.

☞ Set aside an ample chunk of time to do your Fifth Step— three hours at the very least. Although you'll be the one "confessing," you'll very likely find yourself in conversation about events and experiences that ring true for your "confessor." And because this is probably the first time you've been totally, scrupulously honest, it may take an hour or so before you get into the funky flow of telling the unvarnished truth.

## Use Your Sponsor for Your Fifth Step If . . .

- He or she has been your sponsor from the beginning.
- He or she is the one who suggested you complete a Fourth Step inventory.

• He or she won't let you get away with making yourself
seem much better, or infinitely worse, than you are.

## Use Someone Other Than Your Sponsor If . . .

• He or she is out of town or otherwise unavailable.
• This is your second or third go-around, and you are
ready to hear someone else's perspective.
• There are unresolved communication and/or personality
problems between the two of you, and it's not clear who
is going to get fired by whom first.
• You complete a Fourth and Fifth Step while away on a
retreat.
• You just don't want to. (Take a quick inventory of your
motivations for cutting your sponsor out of the privilege
of hearing your Fifth Step.)

☞ Using someone other than your sponsor? That's fine, but
keep in mind that you want someone who
• won't wig out when you reveal your most secret skeevy
stuff
• knows how to keep a confidence and doesn't gossip
• listens carefully and compassionately without needless
interruption
• will be able to mentally organize what you've said into
identifiable patterns of attitude and behavior, then de-
liver those insights respectfully
• has either done a Fourth and Fifth Step of his or her own
or understands the recovery process and the value of
Twelve Step work

☞ Use your written Fourth Step to remind yourself about the
key events and issues you will need to talk about; then start

spilling! In other words, consider your Fourth Step a set of talking points rather than a fully scripted soliloquy.

☞ Make every effort to find a place for your Fifth Step that's comfortable, safe, and private. At home, turn off all telephone ringers, turn down the answering machines, and make sure family traffic doesn't interrupt this important conversation. Choose someplace relatively secluded if you do your Fifth Step outdoors. What you want to do is protect yourself from being distracted and interrupted.

> "Pain is mandatory. Suffering is optional."

☞ Schedule some quiet time after completing your Fifth Step to integrate the experience more fully. Integration is a process of sorting out, "taking in," and making peace. Keep in mind that you will have spent several hours telling the truth about the connection between who you are and what you did — probably for the first time. Therefore, do not plan on going grocery shopping, re-installing all your software, or visiting your aging parents until you've had a long walk, nap, hot bath, or all that and more.

☞ What to do with this document after completing your Fifth Step? Some people advocate ceremonial burning; others recommend keeping it for posterity. If you decide to keep your Fourth Step inventory for future reference, keep it safely stored away from inquiring minds that think they want to know what's in it when, in fact, they would stroke-out if they ever read it.

## The Way Things Were

This version of the Twelve Steps has been floating around the Twelve Step community so long it's now, like the slogans, considered public domain.

"The Twelve Steps to Insanity" could be considered a parody, if it weren't such an accurate depiction of pre-recovery attitudes and behaviors. Take a good long look at it the next time you feel fed up with marching up 'n' down the Twelve Steps. Do you really want to go back to the way things were?

### The Twelve Steps to Insanity

1. We admitted we were powerless over nothing. We could manage our lives perfectly, and we could manage those of anyone else who would allow it.
2. Came to believe that there was no power greater than ourselves, and the rest of the world was insane.
3. Made a decision to have our loved ones and friends turn their wills and their lives over to our care.
4. Made a searching and fearless moral inventory of everyone we knew.
5. Admitted to the whole world at large the exact nature of their wrongs.
6. Were entirely ready to make others straighten up and do right.
7. Demanded that others either "shape up or ship out."
8. Made a list of anyone who had ever harmed us and became willing to go to any length to get even with them all.
9. Got direct revenge on such people whenever possible except when to do so would cost us our own lives or, at the very least, a jail sentence.
10. Continued to take inventory of others, and when they were wrong promptly and repeatedly told them about it.
11. Sought through nagging to improve our relations with others as we couldn't understand them at all, asking only that they knuckle under and do things our way.

12. Having had a complete physical, emotional, and spiritual breakdown as a result of these steps, we tried to blame it on others and to get sympathy and pity in all our affairs.

## Simply Put: Steps Six and Seven

*Six: Were entirely ready to have God remove all these defects of character.*

*Seven: Humbly asked Him to remove our shortcomings.*

Character defects? Previously useful coping mechanisms? Instincts? Whatever. They ain't working, and while you may well be, as they say, "sick and tired of being sick and tired," these two Steps are not about your human ability to excise less-than-useful behaviors. They're about your readiness to let God do the work of transformation. If you still don't buy the God stuff and are not particularly keen about turning anything over to a Higher Power, you're not ready to work these Steps.

Oh drat, more God stuff. To develop a God of your understanding, you'll need to ditch all preconceived religion-based images. Get to know God by going on a date with the Almighty: a walk, cup of coffee, or fireside chat. Explain out loud

> "If God is your copilot, switch seats."

- why you don't believe in God and are skittish about starting
- who or what turned you off to God in the first place
- what your major beefs are: being an addict, coming from a dysfunctional family, unanswered prayers, people who believe in God, and so on

• how you see yourself, how you perceive God, and how
  you perceive your relationship with/to God

Go ahead and have a conniption about what a total crock you
think the God stuff is; be as accusatory as you desire. Name-
calling and blaming might also feel mighty good. Demand proof
of God's existence. Get it all out of your system. After all, the God
of your understanding should be big enough to handle your skep-
ticism, rage, and disappointment, right? Do this as completely and
honestly as you can; then notice if and when the God stuff starts
shifting for you.

☞ Review your Fourth Step inventory to glean which attitudes or behaviors have habitually landed you in trouble with
yourself and others. These are precisely the "character defects"
you'll need to become "entirely ready" to "humbly" ask God to
remove.

☞ Still not sure what constitutes a character defect worthy of
removal? Listen with your inner ear to the inner voice that says
the following:

• This is getting me nowhere.
• Why on earth did I say that?
• What was I thinking when I did that?
• How long can I keep doing this?
• I hate feeling like this.

Basically, anything that leaves you muttering to yourself in these
ways can ultimately be traced to at least one character defect—
and probably to a whole lot more.

☞ Still not sure what constitutes a character defect? See
if you are engaging in any of these fabulously self-defeating
attitudes or behaviors: anger, arrogance, bragging, cheating,

competitiveness, contempt, cynicism, defiance, dishonesty, envy, exaggeration, gossip, grandiosity, greed, impatience, in-tolerance, insecurity, jealousy, laziness, lust, lying, perfectionism, pride, rigid-ity, self-pity, or willfulness . . . to name but a few.

> "If nothing changes, nothing changes."

Surely there is *something* on this list that you are right now in this very moment entirely ready to have removed. Pick one and start with it.

☞ When the notion of becoming "entirely ready" makes you feel nauseated with resistance, pray for willingness. If praying for willingness feels like too much, pray for the willingness to be willing. Take your time. God is ready when you are. And as long as you're praying, ask to be given courage. The kind of change recovery requires is not for the faint of heart.

☞ Enhance your readiness for defect removal by thoroughly and honestly examining why you are not yet ready. Here are some questions to ask yourself:
- What was the payoff for thinking or acting this way?
- Does thinking or acting this way still serve any healthy purpose?
- What do I think will happen if I stop thinking or acting this way?
- Who will I be if I stop thinking or acting this way?

Either write your responses out in your journal or talk them out with your sponsor, spiritual advisor, or counselor. Actually, Fido's floppy ears are indeed an option this time.

☞ Step Six requires a readiness to have all—not merely some—defects of character removed. Nevertheless, you proba-bly feel that some of these "defects" are helpful and appropriate "coping mechanisms" that you are loathe to release. Write a list of the ones you feel like hanging on to for a while, so at least you know what you're choosing.

☛ Resolve to then actually respond differently by doing the complete opposite of what you would have "normally" or "intuitively" done before entering recovery. If, for example, you want to jump into another intimate relationship the moment (or mere months) after one ends, take time off. If you want to go shopping to escape, stay in and feel your feelings. If you want to isolate, go out and be with people. And so forth and so on. . . .

## Think, Think, Think . . . Differently

Lo and behold, a miracle: You are entirely ready to change. You're all geared to let the God of your understanding help you out. Still, you find yourself responding predictably and oh-so-inappropriately to situations. You may be in recovery, but some days your behavior makes it hard to tell. The elapsed time between thought and action is so minimal as to be undetectable. Your responses are automatic, not unlike a starving lab rat in the presence of cheese. Now, everyone is "suggesting" you "do it differently." What does *that* mean?

Time to adopt the principles and techniques of cognitive therapy. Initially developed to treat clinical depression, this therapeutic approach zooms in on all the automatic and negative self-talk that can lead to emotional trouble. Cognitive therapy is perfect for addicts in recovery who are ready to break the cycle of what Twelve Steppers call "stinking thinking."

Cognitive therapy is based on the premise that whatever you "feel" may in fact be a total distortion of reality, some bill of spoiled goods your mind has sold your psyche. Therapists trained in this approach teach clients to first notice the "automatic thoughts" that underlie any uncomfortable emotion (e.g., fear, anxiety, anger, disappointment). They say that teasing out the "cognitive distortions" embedded in those automatic thoughts and developing "rational responses" to them will lead to significant shifts in both mood and behavior.

The ability to identify automatic thoughts is particularly useful when working Steps Six and Seven.

So now what?

Get ready to do more writing! Try following this sequence:

1. Every time you feel emotional discomfort, stop what you're doing to focus on what is running through your mind. (If you can identify the feelings, give yourself a pat on the head. If you can't, maybe you'd better invest in that happy-face poster after all.)

2. Write out every thought, as it occurs to you, about decisions you need to make or actions you need to take.

3. Notice which options hold the most appeal. Notice if this is how you'd "normally" proceed.

4. Do the opposite!

☞ Regard every situation as an opportunity to act "as if" you've already changed your more egregious attitudes and behaviors. Act as if you truly believe honesty is important, gossip is inappropriate, yelling never solved a thing, and sulking doesn't work. Impersonate a "healthy" person at home and at work until you become one.

☞ Create the kinesthetic experience of handing your character defect over to God by scribbling a description of it out on a piece of paper. Fold this note up and drop it into the "God box" you'll create out of an empty tea tin, oatmeal box, or thirty gallon garbage can. Remember to date your note so that when you empty the box out in a few months, you can see what God has indeed removed. (You can also use this box to give God whatever fears continue to plague you.)

"If you always do what you always did, you're going to get what you always got."

☛ How will you know you are changing? Become a scientist in the lab of life! Keep a written log of your behaviors as well as the stimuli that trigger them. No, you don't have to prove your literary worth. Just simply note what bugged you and how you responded, remembering to date the entries. Review this chronological data every few months. Hopefully, over time, you'll shift from wall punching and door slamming to under-the-breath muttering and, ultimately, to praying for whoever ticked you off.

☛ Print the Seventh Step Prayer (see page 76 of the Big Book of AA) on the front of a three-by-five-inch note card:

*My creator, I am now willing*
*that you should have all of me, good and bad.*
*I pray that you now remove from me*
*every single defect of character*
*which stands in the way of my usefulness*
*to you and my fellows.*
*Grant me strength, as I go out from here,*
*to do your bidding.*
*Amen.*

On the back, list all the dysfunctional quirks you're ready for God to remove—and perhaps some you want to keep. Carry this card around in your wallet or purse, whipping it out for a quick read whenever something or someone bugs the living poop out of you.

## Simply Put: Step Eight

*Made a list of all persons we had harmed, and became willing to make amends to them all.*

You're ready to let go of the past and come out of the self-imposed isolation of addiction. By now, you have a pretty good idea of who suffered because of your addiction, so list them. Here's the dicey part: mustering the willingness to set the record right.

☞ Before writing anyone else's name on your Eighth Step list, write your own. In big letters. In your favorite color. Not like you're a victim, but to register the fact that you've harmed your own body, mind, and spirit through addiction.

☞ Whose name goes on your Eighth Step list? Try this meditation: You've finally put some clean and sober time together. Now, imagine yourself strolling down the street . . . or standing in line for an afternoon movie . . . or wandering around the supermarket . . . or sitting at an outdoor cafe sipping a double mocha latte . . . or browsing through a bookstore . . . or casually picking up the phone when it rings.

Suddenly, you catch a glimpse of someone's face . . . or recognize a characteristic walk . . . or hear a familiar voice.

Your body temperature drops ten degrees . . . or the butterflies in your stomach start pounding bongo drums . . . or you feel like keeling over or blowing lunch. *That's* the person whose name goes on your Eighth Step list.

☞ Review the list of your character defects; then travel back in time to pinpoint who suffered physically, emotionally, financially, or spiritually as a result of your pre-recovery adventures. In other words, who has been harmed by your impatience, indifference, arrogance, self-centeredness, habitual lying, and so on? There are probably scads of people you've pissed off. For now, just focus on actual or quantifiable harms (e.g., Whose lives crashed when your wife found those love letters? How much money *did* you swipe by padding your expense account?).

> "Resentments are like drinking poison and waiting for the other person to die."

☞ Cull names for your Eighth Step list from your Fourth Step inventory. At this point, don't worry about whether it's at all possible to make amends or whether making the amends would cause even more grief and pain. Save that sorting for your Ninth Step work.

☞ Think you have a complete list? Go back one more time and add
- everyone you've harmed because you *didn't* do something you were supposed to do
- institutions or organizations, if your pre-recovery exploits include property theft, grand larceny, tax evasion, forgery, or embezzlement

☞ After you generate a comprehensive list of those who deserve to receive amends, it's time to work on the willingness aspect of Step Eight. Divide your list into four columns— "Amends now," "Amends later," "Amends maybe," and "Amends when hell becomes an ice rink"—and distribute names accordingly.

Remember, you are only creating a list at this juncture, so you may as well 'fess up to who, as far as you're concerned in this moment anyway, will never ever receive restitution from you.

## Simply Put: Step Nine

*Made direct amends to such people wherever possible, except when to do so would injure them or others.*

Time to tackle the task of making repairs and restitution without causing any more damage.

☞ Take a look at your Eighth Step list and with the guidance, support, and approval of your sponsor, remove the names of those who would be injured by hearing from you. You can also remove the name of anyone who would be impossible (not just inconvenient) to track down or contact because of changes in name, sex, or residence. Leave dead people on your list.

☞ Time for another chart! Divide a sheet of paper into three columns: "Who I harmed," "What I did," and "What would make it right?" Fortunately, you already have most of the information handy from your Fourth and Eighth Step inventories and should have no problem filling in the first two columns. Your "to do" list for column three might include

- verbal apology, accompanied by behavior change
- direct cash payments, accompanied by behavior change
- donations of time or money to a good cause (i.e., community service), accompanied by behavior change
- a written letter, accompanied by behavior change

An apology is not an amends unless it is accompanied by a real, visible, tangible, quantifiable change in behavior. And because Step Nine says "direct amends . . . wherever possible," you will need to make every effort to do this work face-to-face, getting on planes, trains, boats, and busses as necessary.

☞ Timing is everything, so is having a sense of the appropriate. You want to strike a balance between promptly and prematurely. For example, check with your sponsor about whether your parents' fiftieth wedding anniversary is the proper time and place for a dramatic amends scene four months after you've been sprung from a rehab.

☞ Take a program pal along for the ride when you travel to make particularly nerve-wracking amends. While it is not appropriate to have your friend physically present to hold your hand (or whisper the "right" words in your ear), you'll be happy to have someone there afterward to help you drive home or get to a meeting.

☞ Surround yourself with support as you make difficult amends by calling program pals before you write letters or make phone calls, then after the deed has been done. The first call will help you get centered; the second, debriefed.

☞ Remember the integration time you needed after the intensity of completing Step Five? You'll probably need even more time to fully work through everything that surfaced while you were making Ninth Step amends. This is a very heavy-duty growth process, so schedule amends over a period of months and don't forget to say your prayers along the way.

☞ Keep a copy of your Eighth Step list in your wallet for handy reference and as a reminder not only of what you have to handle, but of your willingness to do so.

☞ Whenever you're unsure about whether making an amends would cause additional harm, hold off until you can discuss motives and expectations with your sponsor and other trusted friends in recovery. This may come as a shock, but when you make amends, you may not be graciously thanked for coming clean. On the other hand, you just might. In either event, you are not responsible for the results.

☞ Remember the slogan "Easy does it"? Start out by making amends that are easy, either because the incident wasn't all that horrible or because the person to whom you are making amends has a generous spirit.

☞ Practice the amends process with other people in recovery. At least they understand what you are doing, why you are doing it, and how difficult amends-making can be. When you're ready for the real thing, walk right up to someone and start by saying, "I owe you an amends." Don't be surprised if at least 50 percent of the time that person has no memory of the event that has been eating at you. This, by the way, doesn't mean not to do it. The amends process is for *your* peace of mind.

☞ Get your amends process off to a good start by owning your stuff! Admit that what you did was wrong, apologize, and then say that you want to make restitution. (If you owe money, be prepared to make the first installment of your payments right then and there.) Depending on the person and circumstances, you may or may not want to talk about your addiction and the fact that you're in recovery. Be mindful that playing the "sick and suffering" addict card may come off as a manipulative bid for sympathy and praise.

Make eye contact with the recipient of your amends. Remember to breathe, even though your heart may be pounding out of your chest. Don't mumble! Try to speak slowly, even if you want to race through your soliloquy as quickly as possible. Keeping in mind that you're unloading a lot of information, some of which may not be received with shouts of joy, give your listener time to really hear what you are saying. And if what you get back is a barrage of accusations and criticism, take a very deep breath and listen. You can process your fresh new crop of resentments later with your sponsor and at a meeting.

☞ Plan to increase your level of meeting attendance, sharing at meetings, and sponsor contact while you work Step Nine. More intense program contact will help offset the scary and stressful nature of amends-making. If you're in therapy, be sure to tell your therapist what you're up to.

☞ Making verbal amends doesn't necessarily have to be a big deal, but if you have a long history of behaving badly without apology, owning up will feel extremely awkward (if not excruciating) at first. Here are some handy phrases to learn and link to the "I'm sorry" everyone ultimately wants to hear:

- I wasn't thinking clearly.
- There's no excuse for what I did (or said), but I do have an explanation if you'd like to hear it.
- What I did (or said) was wrong (or inappropriate).
- I can see now how my behavior hurt you.

Cut everyone (and yourself) a break and do not under any circumstances add these totally unbelievable words, "I swear it will never happen again."

☞ Rather than making verbal amends to people who you know don't realize you've done anything to them, do something special instead. You'll also enhance your credibility as a person in recovery by making "living amends" to anyone who has already heard abundant apologies and prior promises to change. Remember, consistency rebuilds eroded trust. Here are some ways to make living amends:

- Be where you say you will be.
- Do what you say you will do.
- Call ahead if you're going to be late.
- Notice—all by yourself—what needs to be done and pitch in to help.

- Do just a little more than is absolutely necessary.
- Respond without shrugging, sighing, groaning, grunting, muttering, or pulling a face.
- Promptly own your stuff without a lot of dramatic froufrou.
- Offer explanations rather than excuses for screwups.

☞ Better to make amends while those you have harmed are still alive, but what if the person to whom you need to make amends has died? You can still get some psychospiritual relief by writing a long letter owning your part and recognizing how what you did (or didn't do) harmed this person. Read the letter out loud graveside, or before a picture of the dearly departed, or on your knees as a form of prayer to God.

☞ Periodically review your lists to see whether an "Amends later" person has made it onto the "Amends now" list and whether Hell has defrosted for anyone.

## The Promises

There's a huge payoff for working the action Steps that goes way beyond peace of mind. According to the Big Book of AA (pages 83–84), there are "promises" that come true after Step Nine is completed—or at least substantially worked through. And although the promises are part of the AA heritage, anyone who thoroughly and honestly works a Twelve Step program of recovery for any type of addiction is eligible for what might seem like a magical life:

We are going to know a new freedom and a new happiness. We will not regret the past nor wish to shut the door on it. We will comprehend the word serenity and we will know peace. No matter how far down the scale we have gone, we will see how our experience can benefit others. That feeling of uselessness and self-pity will disappear. We will lose interest in selfish things and gain interest in our fellows. Self-seeking will slip away. Our whole attitude and outlook upon life will change. Fear of people and of economic insecurity will leave us. We will intuitively know how to handle situations which used to baffle us. We will suddenly realize that God is doing for us what we could not do for ourselves.

Seem impossible? Check it out with anyone who has already done this work and sustained recovery for any length of time.

## Simply Put: Step Ten

*Continued to take personal inventory and when we were wrong promptly admitted it.*

Telling the truth and making amends has been such a valuable and positive growth experience that you're going to make it a regular part of your lifestyle—especially because you still find yourself acting out even though you're clean, sober, and abstinent.

☞ Take a mini-inventory when

- you first wake up in the morning and plan your day. How will you stay focused on recovery?
- your knickers are in a knot over something that happened at work, at home, at a meeting, while driving, or while allegedly minding your own business.
- someone has the guts to point out that you're acting cranky, mopey, rude, obnoxious, or just plain strange.

- it's the end of the day, after the dog has been walked, cat poop has been scooped, tomorrow's lunch is in the bag, sponsor was called, teeth were brushed, jammies are on—right before you say your prayers and crash out.
- you haven't done one in ages and current events are nipping at your heels.

☞ If you're still not all that keen on making amends, practice self-restraint so you won't have to as often. Cultivate the habit of not immediately banging out irate letters, cursing out diner waitresses, picking up the phone to pitch a fit, or clicking on the reply prompt to flame someone via e-mail. Give yourself at least an hour and use that time to take a quick inventory of what happened and your role in it. You can write this out or talk it out with your sponsor or someone in the program.

> "The road to recovery is always under repair."

☞ Make sure that any inventory you take includes whatever you did right: instances of helping another person, taking the initiative, or modeling the positive effects of working a strong program of recovery.

☞ Be on the lookout for self-righteousness and its sidekick emotion, self-justification. Plan to do a spot-check inventory whenever you catch yourself feeling morally superior or entitled to something.

☞ Examine your motives—before—saying or doing anything for someone else's so-called benefit. Why are you really offering "observations" or "feedback"? Why are you really being so courageously helpful? While you're at it, ask yourself why you'd want others to know about your incredibly long work hours, incredibly responsible job, or incredibly bad migraine.

You'll know you're getting a wee bit more sober when you simply and directly tell people you feel unappreciated, are excited about succeeding, or need a warm hug, cool washcloth, and bowl of chicken soup.

☞ If you haven't bothered trying this, now might be a good time to learn which emotions give rise to actual feeling states in your body. Rapid or uneven heartbeat, shortness of breath, sudden waves of nausea, and feeling goose bumps or "electrical" sensations indicate that something is going on emotionally. At this point in your recovery, consider using this physiological feedback to admit mistakes and wrongs more promptly.

> "Trust God, clean house, and help others."

☞ Almost all religious traditions have some way of marking the day for prayer and contemplation. Traditional Jewish observance designates three times; the Rule of Saint Benedict calls for a sacred pause seven times; and followers of Islam are called to prayer five times throughout the day. Establishing regular breaks during the day to stop and take stock of your attitude, behavior, and spiritual condition will be a powerful support for your continued recovery. At the very least, commit to working Step Eleven ("sought through prayer and meditation") at the endpoints of each day.

☞ Keep a notebook by your bed, and as part of your nightly inventory write a few sentences in response to these questions:

- Was I willing to turn stuff over to God today? Did I even bother making conscious contact with God today?
- Did I have contact with the program today in the form of a meeting, a conversation with my sponsor, or phone contact with someone else in recovery?

- What am I grateful for today? Did I happen to show any gratitude?
- Was I resentful, self-pitying, fearful, or willful?
- What did I learn about myself today?

☞ Rereading your stash of lists, inventories, and journals a few times a year will help you see the bigger picture of your recovery. Do this with soothing music in the background. Make a note to tell your sponsor about the patterns you notice, especially if there has been any slippage in your recovery (e.g., fewer expressions of gratitude, more griping).

## Simply Put: Step Eleven

*Sought through prayer and meditation to improve our conscious contact with God as we understood Him, praying only for knowledge of His will for us and the power to carry that out.*

It's time to develop a more intimate relationship with the God of your understanding by using the time-tested techniques of prayer and meditation. In doing so (or as a result of), you will become more willing to let God be God.

☞ Commit to being on your knees for at least one chat with your Higher Power per day. This much-maligned submissive posture is great for undermining arrogance. Hate the idea of kneeling? Well, did it bother you when you had to search under furniture for drugs that rolled out of reach, rummage under the sink for food you hid on yourself, or knelt before the porcelain god puking your guts out?

☞ If you can't remember to stop for your scheduled prayer time, stash something you need to get going in the morning underneath your bed at night. As long as you're already down there fishing around for car keys or eyeglasses, you may as well pray.

☞ What is the longest period of time that you can imagine meditating? Ten minutes? How about five? One minute? Even one minute is better than zero minutes. Set the timer on your watch, microwave, or alarm clock for sixty seconds; then sit in meditation. Gradually increase the amount of tolerable time until you reach fifteen to twenty minutes. (Longtime, heavy-duty meditators can sit for hours. Don't you try this without sober adult supervision.)

## Sitting Meditation Made Easier

Okay, so you already know that meditation is a revered practice in both Western and Eastern spiritual traditions. You also know that mainstream health practitioners recognize meditation as an effective way to reduce stress, lower blood pressure, and relax muscular tension.

Yet, in your experience, sitting meditation feels lousy. At several points during your recovery process you tried it and were jumping out of your skin within nanoseconds. News flash from the Spiritual Technique Front: You don't have to sit to meditate.

It's not that you did it wrong. In fact, there's growing agreement among meditation researchers that sitting meditation is not particularly helpful for anyone suffering from anxiety or depression, both of which are present during the restless, unstable years of early recovery. In part, this is because sitting meditation often uncovers what led to addiction in the first place, and *that* may be much too icky to sit with early on.

If you've rejected sitting meditation because it felt like

"too much," you've simply discovered this bit of wisdom on your own. Your body/mind told you that sitting meditation is not for you—not now, anyway. But don't give up entirely. There are other forms of meditation.

All forms of meditation help quiet "mind chatter" so that together, body and mind can release into deeper relaxation. As the body/mind relaxes, deeper tensions—both physical and emotional—surface, which is why people feel antsy.

Meditation, a key yogic practice, also helps practitioners become more conscious. You'll know you've developed this when you're able to see what you're doing with heightened awareness. After settling into a regular meditation practice, you should begin to notice an increased clarity about life events—especially challenging ones—and your role in them. (Count on your Fourth and Tenth Steps getting very juicy!)

You can also receive these great benefits from practicing styles of meditation involving movement, sound, or contemplation.

Walking, hatha yoga, and "trance dance" are somewhat obvious forms of "meditation in motion," but so are activities such as knitting, cooking, dish washing, and auto detailing. Singing, chanting, and toning are ways to meditate using sound. Focusing on a candle flame, devotional art, a word or phrase from sacred literature, or your big toe qualify as contemplative forms of meditation. *Basically, anything you do with intentionality qualifies as meditation.* The point is to engage in something so completely that your mind shuts up long enough to give the peace that passes all understanding a chance to sally forth.

☞ Create a special setting for your regular time of prayer and meditation. This can be the corner of a room, a section of your desk, your dresser top, the bathtub—with or without water. The objective is to find and establish a place where you can get personal and vocal with God. Make it sacred with props such as candles, flowers, favorite pictures, selections from your miniature car collection, and the like.

> "Religion is for people who are afraid they'll go to hell. Spirituality is for people who have been there."

☞ Use the principle "One day at a time" to get used to praying and/or meditating regularly. In other words, renew your commitment to make "conscious contact" with God each day instead of burying yourself under the perceived burden of "having to do this forever."

☞ Another slogan, "Keep it simple," is very handy when praying. Instead of giving the Almighty a list of marching orders to fix your life and, perhaps more important, everyone else in it, pray: "Your will, not mine, be done."

Other simple prayers:

- Help.
- I don't know what to pray.
- You're in charge.
- Please help me understand your will for my life.
- Thank you.

☞ Actively seek out opportunities for "corporate" prayer and meditation. This can be done by attending a synagogue or church; sitting *zazen* with a bona-fide *Roshi;* attending a regular, spiritually oriented yoga class; or gathering more informally with a group in someone's rumpus room. There is something especially enlivening about acknowledging the presence of a Higher Power in a group setting. It's a powerful complement to solo spiritual practices.

☛ Your program of recovery should enhance your formal religious/ spiritual commitments and vice versa. Stay away from any organized group that demands you choose it over your Twelve Step program. Why limit your peace, serenity, and salvation to a particular expression of piety?

> "God answers *every* prayer and sometimes the answer is 'no.'"

☛ Take whatever revelations you've allegedly received during your spiritual practices and instead of rushing forth to allegedly help someone else, use this Divine information to pray for God's will in that person's life.

☛ A twofer: Get in some spiritual practices plus spend quality time with your kids by reading to them out of prayer and meditation books as a bedtime treat. They'll appreciate having conscious contact with you, and you'll be taking care of yourself at the same time. Note: This only works with younger children. You'll probably want to have a chunk of recovery time and possibly some therapy before attempting this level of communion with teenagers, especially ones who remember you at the height/ depth of your addiction.

## Prayer 101

Although they are complementary ways to establish conscious contact with God, prayer and meditation are not the same spiritual enterprise. Unlike meditation which is introspective, prayer is interactive. Some explain it like this: Prayer is speaking to God; meditation is listening.

If you're a talker (and even if you're not), the benefits of prayer make it well worth overcoming any initial weirdness you may feel about blathering on to what looks to be nothing but a severely depleted ozone layer.

Here are some tips for getting started:

**Get un-embarrassed.** Most people feel strange when they start staking out the turf of faith by talking to God. After all, there are clinical labels for people who do this sort of thing. If it's any consolation, the greatest saints and spiritual masters have always been viewed as loony by their contemporaries. Although talking out loud to God may initially propel you out of the comfort zone, it will eventually land you in another.

**Get inspired.** Until you find your own devotional voice, feel free to rely on formal prayers for inspiration. Snippets of psalms and, if you were raised as a Christian, the Lord's Prayer are probably already data-based in your brain from childhood. You can find others in one of the gazillion prayer anthologies currently available.

After you prime the prayer pump, you'll undoubtedly find yourself moved to pray while walking outside in nature, gazing at mountains, or watching the cat snooze in a patch a sunlight. You can also find oodles of inspiration in less glorious situations such as being stopped by cops, waiting for mammogram results, or getting sued for divorce. Inspiration is everywhere, once you start looking.

**Get diligent.** Like recovery itself, prayer deserves diligence. You don't even have to want to pray; going through the motions can build a surprising level of comfort. Try this: Pray to believe in prayer until you believe in prayer.

**Get real.** Unless your prayer sounds like a list of terrorist demands, it's almost impossible to pray wrong. This is a heartfelt activity, not a cognitive one. Your prayer doesn't have to be delivered in eloquent, neo-King Jamesian English or start with traditional salutations like "Gracious God" or "Heavenly Father." It doesn't even have to make sense.

Skip the oratory and simply have a simple conversation with the most generous, loving, nonjudgmental, compassionate listener in all existence. (That *is* the God of your understanding, right?) Simply clear your throat and say, "Well God, here I am again" and let the rest of the words choose you.

☞ Pick an established written prayer and memorize it. (Start with a short or familiar one from your childhood.) Then, memorize another. And another. And another. The point is to build a repertory of inspiration so that you have something to draw upon when your heart feels dry.

> "Be careful about what you pray for—you just might get it."

☞ Enliven your conscious contact with God by taking a spiritually oriented retreat. Early on, try to find a retreat that's organized and led around Twelve Step principles. After you log more recovery time and have developed a regular spiritual practice, you can look into more generic spiritual retreat centers. Ask around for suggestions, wander the www.world, or pick up a published guide to retreat centers.

☞ Harkening back to the Sixth and Seventh Steps, notice when things in your life become particularly complex, messy, stupid, and annoying. View this as Divine Evidence that you're out of alignment with God's will. You can quickly remedy this by praying for the knowledge of God's will and the strength and grace to carry it out. Of course, you also have to commit to paying attention to whatever Divine clues, no matter how subtle, float by. You'll know that whatever post-prayer action you take is right when you feel utterly serene, as if relieved of a heavy burden. Still feeling odd? Go back to praying to know God's will.

> "Everything you do is a step toward recovery or toward relapse."

☞ Combine spiritual fitness with physical fitness by using your walking or running time to pray or listen to inspirational tapes.

Note: This technique is not particularly effective for team sports. Never mind how many pro football teams claim pregame prayer groups, "Please God, let us slaughter them" is not in alignment with the theory of Step Eleven.

## Simply Put: Step Twelve

*Having had a spiritual awakening as the result of these steps, we tried to carry this message to [others in the same boat], and to practice these principles in all our affairs.*

At long last, you're ready to expand your understanding and practice of the Twelve Steps to the rest of your life. In doing so, you will carry their message to those who have as yet to be delivered from the bondage of addiction.

☞ You'll know that you've had a spiritual awakening when you notice yourself

- turning to God as a first, rather than last, resort in both good times and bad
- taking action after, instead of before, receiving both natural and supernatural guidance
- wanting to respond differently to people and events you previously considered great excuses to drink, drug, eat, gamble, shop, smoke, and so on
- accepting that recovery is a process, not an event
- feeling more awake and aware, joyful, generous, honest, hopeful, open, patient, and willing

☞ "Carry the message" by serving others which, surprise, surprise, is covered in the very next chapter of this book.

# 5

## Helping Others

Don't let the positioning of this chapter as last fool you into thinking that "service" is less important than any other program-related task. Even the person with only one day of clean time performs a mighty service to others simply by showing up. As you acquire more "twenty-fours," your concept and practice of service will deepen.

This service biz is not about asking, "Paper or plastic?" Serving others is ultimately about moving from self to Self and beyond.

Twelve Step programs are very big on helping others, for a variety of reasons. First, there's the self-absorption thing—a prime feature of the addictive personality; add to that other identifiable character traits such as impulsivity and selfishness. The person who once hoarded pills, bounced checks to cover losses, and maintained a private stash of vodka in the underwear drawer now, in early recovery, thinks nothing of reaching across a crowded table to take the very last scoop of mashed potatoes. Serving others—literally and figuratively—helps to break the continuous loop of self-absorption.

As a prime feature of recovery, helping others is also extremely practical. After all, how much trouble can you possibly get into while helping newcomers find meetings, going on speaking commitments, and setting up meeting rooms? Become a useful, productive member of your Twelve Step fellowship, and sooner or later you'll become a useful, productive member of society at large. The tips in this chapter suggest ways to accomplish this amazing feat.

Last, but certainly not least, the emphasis on serving others is yet more evidence that you are participating not in a self-help program, but in a spiritual one.

Every great, enduring spiritual tradition views service to others as an essential feature of spiritual growth. Every Twelve Step program views service to others as essential for continued recovery. Surprise, surprise: The process of spiritual growth and the process of recovery are nearly identical. This makes complete sense if you believe that, in addition to being "an allergy of the body" and "an abnormality of the mind," addiction is a manifest form of soul sickness. (This doesn't yet make sense? Stick around until it does!)

If you're serious about recovery, you'll eventually have to get serious about helping others on a regular basis. Over time, you'll find yourself doing this less grudgingly and more happily. Eventually, selfless service will become as essential to your Being as the air you breathe. You may never be cured, but you will be healed.

## CHAPTER TIPS

☞ Intensify your commitment to Twelve Step service work whenever you are feeling sorry for yourself, are bummed by the recovery process, aren't sponsoring anyone, or think you are much too busy living your life to bother with meetings.

☞ When you arrive at a meeting, keep an eye out for befuddled newcomers and head for them first instead of your buddies. Even if the meeting has official "greeters," introduce yourself, offer a cup of coffee (with or without apologies for its quality), and perhaps introduce them to others. After the meeting is over, remember to bid them adieu with a gracious and heartfelt "Keep coming back."

☞ Even if you don't officially volunteer to set up or clean up, when the request is made, pitch in to help anyway.

☞ Serve the community of those in recovery, those who need to be, and yourself by doing the following:

• Ask for help when you need it.
• Be reliable.
• Clean up your stuff promptly.

☞ For a week, month, or longer make it your business to smile at and say hello to people you cannot stand for whatever reason. You don't have to make an effusive big deal out of doing this. Consider it a tangible act of placing "principles over personalities."

☞ Being at a meeting—whether you speak or not—counts as service. Just think about how it would affect a newcomer if everyone stayed home.

☞ Make yourself known to the "powers that be" at the nearest rehab or outpatient program as someone who is willing to provide rides to meetings.

If and when it feels right, let your priest, pastor, minister, or rabbi know you're available as a resource to other congregants. At some point you might even want to let the employee assistance program (EAP) folks at work use you as a contact person for troubled colleagues.

☞ Before volunteering, take an inventory of your talents to assess whether your abilities mesh with the demands of the position. Then have a conversation with yourself, God, and an-

**"You have to give it away to keep it."**

other person (sound familiar?) about whether you're ready to be catapulted into a situation that requires a more intense level of accountability, such as handling money, representing your group at the state level, or ordering literature.

☛ Use all service activities—especially at the group level—to keep hacking away at the defects of character you uncovered in Step Six. Don't be surprised if chairing meetings, organizing anniversary meetings, or making sure there are enough cookies with chocolate brings out pride, self-righteousness, fear, grandiosity, self-centeredness, impatience, and any other pesky traits you'd be better off without.

☛ When, for the first time in your recovery history, someone (finally) asks you to be a sponsor, hold off on saying "yes" or "no" until you check with yours. Even after you have a few years of recovery, it's a good idea to check it out. Addicts tend to believe that more is better in *all* situations. It ain't.

### You'll Know You're Ready to Sponsor Someone When . . .

- You are asked.
- Your sponsor says you are.
- The prospect of sponsoring someone is simultaneously exciting and terrifying.

### You're Not Ready to Sponsor Anyone If . . .

- You think you *should* be asked because you are working such a fabulous program.

- You haven't quite yet gotten around to working Steps Four and Five.
- You don't have a sponsor and/or think meetings are a waste of time.

☞ After you get the go-ahead from your sponsor to sponsor someone else, pick a newcomer from the lineup and volunteer to be a temporary sponsor.

☞ Periodically review all service activities to make sure you have a balance among types (e.g., formal and informal, group and one-to-one) and between giving and receiving. Also, take a look at the amount of time you spend on service as opposed to sleeping, eating, keeping in conscious contact with the God of your understanding, and continuously working the Steps. These activities are what will allow you to be sober enough to serve.

> **"You can carry the message, but not the person."**

☞ Establish and maintain clear boundaries around service work. Offer to help someone fill out a loan application instead of lending money. Accompany someone to look for a place to rent instead of inviting him or her to move right into your home. Step aside and let someone else take over instead of volunteering (or being volunteered) to perform the same group service tasks year after year.

## At Your Service

Despite its undisputed Christian origins, Twelve Step programs reflect the values of many other great world religions.

Check out, for example, Judaism's concept of *tzedakah*, or "charitable giving," which is an activity that certainly qualifies as a form of service.

During the twelveth century, this long-standing Jewish value was organized into a hierarchy by perhaps the greatest Jewish philosopher and codifier of Jewish law, Moses Maimonides. This centuries-old guideline is well worth keeping in mind as you cultivate a life of service to others today.

Maimonides came up with eight degrees of giving, each of greater spiritual purity than the last:

1. To give grudgingly, reluctantly, or with regret.
2. To give less than we should, but with grace.
3. To give what one should, but only after being asked.
4. To give before one is asked.
5. To give without knowing who will receive it, although the recipient knows the identity of the giver.
6. To give without making known one's identity.
7. To give so that neither giver nor recipient knows the identity of the other.
8. To help another to become self-supporting, by means of a gift, a loan, or by finding employment for the one in need.

Going on speaking commitments is a powerful way to do Twelve Step service work. They're called "commitments" to remind you to follow through on your promise to show up. Speaking commitments will support your recovery if you

- say "yes" whenever you're asked to speak, unless you're physically unable to do so.
- participate at a variety of environments such as open meetings, correctional facilities, and rehabilitation units.
- go along even if you don't have a speaking role. Your presence will support those from your group who do speak.

- travel with the group instead of taking your own car. You'll end up with a meeting in the car on the way, a meeting at your destination, and a meeting on the way home—three meetings for the effort of one!

## Once Upon a Time . . .

Like so many other things, the popular expression "What's your story?" suddenly takes on new meaning after you become part of the Twelve Step community. The speaking commitment is an opportunity to tell the true-life action adventure story of your addiction. The benefits of doing this are abundant.

Talking frankly and honestly about addiction out loud has been at the foundation of recovery ever since Bill W. spilled his guts about needing a drink to Dr. Bob. It doesn't matter how much your story changes over time—and it will, as you remember more and more. What matters is that you hear yourself talk about what you did and didn't do as a result of your addiction. Speaking the "truth" of your own struggle functions to keep you relatively awake and aware while allowing others in recovery to understand that they do, indeed, belong to a community.

So, how to do this?

First, don't bother with note cards or flip charts because you'll be speaking from your heart rather than your mind. (Okay, okay, you may write notes on cards but then leave them home.) Cheery news: Experienced public speakers as well as neophytes initially panic about the thought of talking without props. Everyone gets over it and survives.

Second, there happens to be a suggested format that will help you organize your thoughts. You don't have to get fancy, just focus on

- what it was like (pre-recovery)
- what happened (to persuade you to quit whatever was wrecking your life)
- what it's like now (that you're in recovery)

Keeping this outline in mind will hopefully prevent you from droning on about everything since conception that you so very deeply feel caused your addiction. You'll know if you're speaking too long when people start checking their watches and sneaking out for more coffee.

Finally, remember that you're sharing your "experience, strength, and hope" so that others may benefit. More specifically, this means that while endless "war stories" about your losing battles with addiction may be entertaining for the troops, it's vitally important that you talk about how your life has changed and improved since you up and enlisted in recovery.

Bonus gift: In addition to being perhaps the most effective means of sustaining long-term recovery, Twelve Step programs manage to transform even the most tongue-tied members into amazingly articulate, amusing, and effective public speakers.

☞ Women take note: Be mindful of the audience whenever you tell your story, omitting certain details or episodes when speaking to mixed groups. Sharing the specifics of sexual promiscuity, abuse, commerce, or violence may end up making you feel more vulnerable than you expect or need to be and would perhaps better be saved for therapy.

☞ Keep a supply of area meeting lists and copies of program literature handy to share with others at a moment's notice.

☞ Although the Twelve Traditions provide an excellent control against abuses of authority and power in Twelve Step programs, they don't stop human beings from being human. Check your motivations before

- volunteering to serve in any "official" capacity at the group, local, area, or beyond levels. Is your participation about serving or being recognized?
- having a fit and demanding a "group conscience" meeting because something is, in your opinion, horribly wrong. Is your concern about serving or being recognized?
- jamming your dance card with commitments to speak at or chair meetings, prison visits, sponsees, Twelve Step calls, and ad hoc acts of compulsive generosity. Is your active presence about serving or being recognized?

## Incoming Wounded

Around the month of October, the wags in AA add this commentary to their usual sharing: "Alcoholism is a threefold disease—Thanksgiving, Christmas, and New Year's." Thanks to the stress of these family-oriented holidays, the same could be said for drugging, overeating, smoking, shopping, and that perennial favorite among addicts— codependency.

Ah, the holidays . . . shopping, cooking, travel, entertaining, meals with the extended brood, neighborhood get-togethers, religious services, office parties, the opportunity to review the past year. It's enough to fling non-addicts into the arms of substance abuse. For those who really do have a problem, holidays can be positively lethal.

All this is to say that Twelve Step fellowships usually

harvest a bumper crop of newcomers during and after the winter holidays. (In the summer, look for newcomers after Memorial Day and Fourth of July picnic-brawls.) Not only do these times provide service opportunities galore, but they also give you many occasions to feel a rush of gratitude for your own recovery.

☞ Open your home and set a place at your holiday table for someone (especially a newcomer) who cannot and probably should not go anywhere near blood relatives. By the way, including this person in family-oriented chores like table setting, clearing, or dish washing is being graciously inclusive rather than inhospitable.

☞ Help gather people together for clean, sober, and abstinent alternatives to occasions for slippage by hosting events such as
- football nights or poker games that focus on banter rather than betting and booze
- New Year's Eve dinners that emphasize healthy foods in moderate amounts as opposed to cholesterol-laden repasts and killer chocolate desserts
- late afternoon teas instead of cocktail parties

☞ Volunteering extra service at hospitals, rehabs, or homeless shelters during the winter holiday season not only helps others but also is a great way to experience a motherlode of humility and gratitude.

## The Coffee Commitment

Never mind that caffeine is a powerful nervous-system stimulant with its own significant addictive qualities. If you didn't drink coffee before coming into recovery, you'll probably start. If you already drink coffee, plan on drinking more whether you eventually switch to decaf or not. It's practically a spiritual axiom that when people in recovery get very cranky, it's because there's no coffee readily available. The "coffee commitment" is therefore one of the most important service activities anyone in recovery can perform. It's right up there with carrying the message through speaking; some might argue that one cannot occur without the other.

Afraid of doing it all wrong? Too proud to beg for help? Here's a set of generic directions for brewing coffee.

1. Procure coffee and filters. This is a Twelve Step fellowship not a hip little bistro, so buy whatever happens to be on sale.

2. Procure something that measures at least a tablespoon because you'll need two per three-quarters cup of water. A regulation coffee scoop measures two tablespoons and get this:

    1 tablespoon = 3 teaspoons
    2 tablespoons = 1 fluid ounce

Keep this in mind for emergency situations, like when someone has used the coffee scoop for an ashtray and all you can find are those little white plastic teaspoons that come with soup-to-go. (Can you see why some people find the coffee commitment nerve wracking?)

3. Take a look at the coffee-making equipment.

    If it's a percolator, measure three-quarters cup of cold water per cup of coffee into the percolator, plug it in, and let the water come to a boil. Meanwhile, measure two level tablespoons of coffee per cup into the basket. If the water doesn't boil, make sure you've connected the wire to the

**"Pass it on."** plug outlet on the pot as well as the one on the wall. When the water boils, pour it in the basket, cover it, and let it percolate for six to eight minutes.

If it's an automatic drip contraption, pour cold water into the carafe up to the marked fill line. Put a filter in the basket and start spooning coffee in at a ratio of two level tablespoons per cup.

If the cup level scale has worn off, assume the carafe holds twelve cups even though it might only hold ten cups. Don't worry, for every person who chokes on the coffee, there's another grateful recovering someone who thinks it's fab. Make sure the filled filter basket is in place before pouring anything into the water reservoir. Also, make sure the machine is turned on. (There should be an indicator light somewhere.)

4. Stand watch to make sure that the pot is always almost full, the carafe or pot is thoroughly cleaned after the meeting, and used grounds are tossed out (unless someone wants them for a compost heap).

You'll probably also be in charge of making sure there's enough milk, sugar, sugar substitute, and stirrers. You may also be in charge of cookies and/or crackers. If you think this is a bush-league form of service, volunteer for it and then forget to show up without providing a substitute.

☛ Say "no" to service work when you're physically exhausted, spewing forth influenza (or worse) germs, or have been doing so much that others (or you) mistakenly believe you're in charge.

In the Step Seven spirit of "doing it differently," experiment with saying "no" if you have a history of pathologically agreeing to anything and everything you're asked to do. Check with your sponsor before adopting either strategy.

☞ It doesn't matter which Twelve Step program you're in, make sure you have company whenever you go out on a Twelve Step call: a call on someone in the throes of drinking or drugging or someone who has just landed in the hospital or in jail. This is for your own safety and sanity in the event you encounter violence, hysteria, or unpleasant bodily fluids. There is also the possibility, however remote, that the person you intend to help ends up dragging you down.

☞ Stock up on spiritual ammo by praying for the knowledge of God's will and the power to carry it out before heading off on a Twelve Step call. This will also help you manage your expectations that someone, because of your presence, will fall gratefully to his or her knees and beg to be taken immediately to a Twelve Step meeting.

☞ No matter how desperately you may want to, avoid the very real and possibly overwhelming impulse to "Twelve Step" family members. You're way too emotionally involved. What you can do is exemplify the glories of recovery and turn the person you love over to the care of God—over and over again.

## The Twelfth Tradition

*Anonymity is the spiritual foundation of all our traditions, ever reminding us to place principles before personalities.*

Besides reinforcing the ongoing spiritual practice of humility, there are some very practical reasons for keeping your mouth shut about participating in a specifically named Twelve Step program: social stigma, skittish employers, and the possibility that you may not, in fact, (yet) be the greatest living poster child for recovery.

Nevertheless, as the Byrds sang in the sixties, "to every thing there is a season." (If you don't remember the Byrds, you may recall this from the Book of Ecclesiastes.) There will be times when it is appropriate, useful, and perhaps even necessary to break your anonymity.

Please note, this is about revealing to others the nature of *your* addiction and *your* participation in a Twelve Step program. If there is any unanimity about anonymity, it's that no one has the right to break someone else's cover. In fact, most meeting formats include the reading of an "anonymity statement" to remind people to keep whatever they hear "in the rooms."

Under what circumstances could you be moved to break your anonymity? Here are two of the most typical:

• You observe a friend or colleague in the process of crash landing and believe your story will provide some measure of comfort and hope.

• You are in the process of making amends to someone who is clueless as to why you pulled the spooky stunts you once did.

What if you're summoned by the reigning queen of television talk shows to crusade against alcohol and substance abuse? (You should only be so lucky as to get this chance to place principles before personalities!) Well, first find out whether the network will cover all your expenses for transportation and accommodations. Make sure they agree to handle makeup and hair. Then go!

*Don't* talk about specific Twelve Step programs and your participation. *Don't* mention that you've been wandering in and out of the Alcoholics Anonymous club at the corner of Windmill and Tulip for the past twenty years.

*Do* plan to wax on about the dreadful and life-leeching aspects of addiction that you, thank God, are conquering one day at a time.

☞ Once you get stabilized financially (if not before), add the following items to your list of annual charitable contributions:

"Walk your talk."

- your recovery fellowship at the local, area, or national level
- state or national organizations that conduct research and/or provide education about substance abuse
- halfway houses, treatment centers, or programs that survive on funding and donations

☞ Either officially or unofficially, commit a percentage of your *pro bono* services to indigent members of your recovery fellowship who need legal, medical, or financial advice.

If your talents lie in the disciplines of advertising or public relations, volunteer to write press releases and newsletters or to create public awareness and fund-raising campaigns for local alcoholism and addiction councils.

Have a knack for entertainment? Help organize clean and sober events for the recovery community such as dances, benefit concerts, and gatherings at coffee houses featuring local talent.

☞ Get involved with legislative activities such as letter writing, lobbying, or fund-raising for initiatives that toughen restrictions on driving under the influence, possessing controlled substances, and smoking in public places; levy taxes or surcharges on the purchase of alcohol and nicotine products; and provide funding for treatment and rehabilitation programs.

☞ Notice a sudden rash of drunk driving reports and drug busts hitting the news? Write a letter to the editor that educates people about the available alternatives to jail, insanity, or death.

☞ Volunteer to organize meals for housebound members who need food in addition to the spiritual sustenance provided by meetings.

☞ Talk with your sponsor and those on your phone list that you call regularly for support about expanding the concept—and practical activity—of service beyond the rooms of your Twelve Step fellowship. Review the part of Step Twelve that says to "practice these principles in all our affairs." Ask yourself the following questions:

- What would service look like at work in the community at large or where I formally worship?
- Where else in my life can I be of service?

After all, in recovery, you now have not only a life, but one worth living!

☞ And so, to paraphrase one of the more familiar Twelve Step texts, this compilation of tips for working a Twelve Step program of recovery now comes to a close. But not without trotting out the text of the well-worn and much-loved Serenity Prayer\*:

*God, grant me the serenity*
*to accept the things I cannot change,*
*the courage to change the things I can,*
*and the wisdom to know the difference.*

---

\* This is the "short" version of the Prayer for Serenity attributed to Reinhold Niebuhr. The "long" version that, for reasons that should become obvious, is rarely recited at meetings, goes like this:

God,
grant me the serenity
to accept the things I cannot change,
courage to change the things I can,
and wisdom to know the difference.
Living one day at a time,
enjoying one moment at a time.
Accepting hardship as a pathway to peace.
Taking, as Jesus did, this sinful world as it is,
not as I would have it.
Trusting that You will make all things right
if I surrender to Your will.
So that I may be reasonably happy in this life
and supremely happy with You forever in the next.
Amen.

# Appendixes

# Appendix A
## "Identify but Don't Compare" Film Festival

Is your memory turning a bit brown at the edges? At a loss for fun things to do in recovery? Pop some corn, buy a case of seltzer, stock up on tissues, and invite the clean crowd over to watch Hollywood's view of addiction and recovery.

Notice how each movie portrays the progressive nature of addiction, the patterns of denial, the utter pathos of codependency, and the hope that emerges after the drama of hitting bottom.

### THE LOST WEEKEND

*Ray Milland*
*Jane Wyman*
*MCA Home Video*
*Black and white/100 minutes*
*Best picture of 1945!*

Ray Milland plays a wanna-be writer whose descent into alcoholism culminates in a three-day binge. Jane Wyman is the loyal, codependent girlfriend who is determined to save her man. Included are great gritty portrayals of the role siblings, bartenders, pawn-shop proprietors, and landladies play in aiding and abetting alcoholism, despite their thinly veiled disgust.

While some of the special effects in the DT's scene are a bit hokey by today's high-tech standards, they do not detract from the enduring impact of this film classic—nor does the somewhat implausible ending. (Detox and recovery should only be so easy!)

## DAYS OF WINE AND ROSES

*Jack Lemmon*
*Lee Remick*
*Warner Home Video*
*Black and white/134 minutes*
*1962*

Jack Lemmon is a public relations flack who graciously opens the alcoholism door for good girl Lee Remick whose first yummy Brandy Alexander leads absolutely nowhere good. For every person who has balked at the prospect of detox after seeing Lemmon's character rave and writhe in four-point restraints, there are probably a few who opt for recovery because of Jack Klugman's performance as the AA guy.

This is the quintessential portrayal of what happens in a marriage when one spouse wants to sober up and the other simply doesn't. The closing soliloquy still rings heart-wrenchingly true. Nearly four decades later, this movie still packs an emotional wallop. Plan on crying. Both Lemmon and Remick received Oscar nominations for their performances in this movie.

## CLEAN AND SOBER

*Michael Keaton*
*Warner Home Video*
*Color/124 minutes*
*1988*

Michael Keaton is a real-estate demi-tycoon in a whole lot of trouble, thanks to his increasing fondness and need for nose candy. He decides to hide out in a twenty-one-day detox program where, after being quite the smart-ass, he finally starts to realize that he is indeed an addict. Early recovery is one sad hard lesson after another, probably because this character doesn't follow suggestions. The film is more thought-provoking than emotionally wringing, depending on your current stage of recovery.

## WHEN A MAN LOVES A WOMAN

*Andy Garcia*
*Meg Ryan*
*Touchstone Home Video*
*Color/126 minutes*
*1994*

Andy Garcia and Meg Ryan play a hip, hot-for-each-other couple who have it all: careers, a gorgeous home, two adorable daughters, and a housekeeper. They also have her alcoholic progression and his escalating control, cleverly disguised as "helpfulness."

Ryan's character finally (and literally) crashes to bottom in a harrowing scene that shows how alcoholism is indeed a family disease that marks kids for life. As she sobers up through AA, the husband (Garcia) comes to understand—and own—his part in the recovery dance. Haul out your hankies for Ryan's speaking commitment performance.

## DRUNKS

*Peter Cohn*
*Richard Lewis*
*Faye Dunaway*
*Spalding Gray*
*Howard Rollins*
*Parker Posey*
*Dianne Wiest*
*Amanda Plummer*
*Calista Flockhart*
*BMG Independent*
*Color/88 minutes*
*1995*

A typical meeting of Alcoholics Anonymous, complete with church basement decor and weirdly fascinating soliloquies, is presented by an all-star cast (although this is not a Hollywood production). Comedian Richard Lewis is cast against type in a dramatic role and gives a convincing performance as a grieving widower. In fact, the content and pacing of this screenplay is so realistic that it's probably worth owning a copy to watch if you desperately need a meeting—any meeting—at two o'clock in the morning. In such an instance, forget about popcorn and be sure to sip coffee out of a Styrofoam cup.

**STUART SAVES HIS FAMILY**
  *Al Franken*
  *Laura San Giacomo*
  *Paramount*
  *Color/97 minutes*
  *1995*

Al Franken stretches his original *Saturday Night Live* role as a revoltingly optimistic self-help expert into a feature-length comedy about dysfunctional families.

After his perky television show has been canceled, Stuart Smalley (Franken) heads home to his family which has it all: alcoholism, overeating, codependency. You should probably hold off on watching this ridiculous send-up until you have approximately two years in recovery. By then, hopefully, you'll have developed a sense of humor about the utter absurdity of perpetuating lethal behaviors. If this movie offends you, call your sponsor immediately and increase your meeting attendance exponentially.

# Appendix B

# The Twelve Steps of Various Groups

**The Twelve Steps of Alcoholics Anonymous**

1. We admitted we were powerless over alcohol—that our lives had become unmanageable.
2. Came to believe that a Power greater than ourselves could restore us to sanity.
3. Made a decision to turn our will and our lives over to the care of God *as we understood Him.*
4. Made a searching and fearless moral inventory of ourselves.
5. Admitted to God, to ourselves, and to another human being the exact nature of our wrongs.
6. Were entirely ready to have God remove all these defects of character.
7. Humbly asked Him to remove our shortcomings.
8. Made a list of all persons we had harmed, and became willing to make amends to them all.
9. Made direct amends to such people wherever possible, except when to do so would injure them or others.
10. Continued to take personal inventory and when we were wrong promptly admitted it.
11. Sought through prayer and meditation to improve our conscious contact with God *as we understood Him,* praying only for knowledge of His will for us and the power to carry that out.
12. Having had a spiritual awakening as the result of these steps, we tried to carry this message to alcoholics, and to practice these principles in all our affairs.

The Twelve Steps of AA are taken from *Alcoholics Anonymous,* 3d ed., published by AA World Services, Inc., New York, N.Y., 59–60. Reprinted with permission of AA World Services, Inc. (See author's note on copyright page.)

## The Twelve Steps of Narcotics Anonymous

1. We admitted that we were powerless over our addiction, that our lives had become unmanageable.
2. We came to believe that a Power greater than ourselves could restore us to sanity.
3. We made a decision to turn our will and our lives over to the care of God *as we understood Him.*
4. We made a searching and fearless moral inventory of ourselves.
5. We admitted to God, to ourselves, and to another human being the exact nature of our wrongs.
6. We were entirely ready to have God remove all these defects of character.
7. We humbly asked Him to remove our shortcomings.
8. We made a list of all persons we had harmed, and became willing to make amends to them all.
9. We made direct amends to such people wherever possible, except when to do so would injure them or others.
10. We continued to take personal inventory and when we were wrong promptly admitted it.
11. We sought through prayer and meditation to improve our conscious contact with God *as we understood Him,* praying only for knowledge of His will for us and the power to carry that out.
12. Having had a spiritual awakening as the result of these steps, we tried to carry this message to addicts, and to practice these principles in all our affairs.

## The Twelve Steps of Gamblers Anonymous

1. We admitted we were powerless over gambling—that our lives had become unmanageable.
2. Came to believe that a Power greater than ourselves could restore us to a normal way of thinking and living.
3. Made a decision to turn our will and our lives over to the care of this Power of our own understanding.
4. Made a searching and fearless moral and financial inventory of ourselves.
5. Admitted to ourselves and to another human being the exact nature of our wrongs.
6. Were entirely ready to have these defects of character removed.
7. Humbly asked God (of our understanding) to remove our shortcomings.
8. Made a list of all persons we had harmed and became willing to make amends to them all.
9. Made direct amends to such people wherever possible, except when to do so would injure them or others.
10. Continued to take personal inventory and when we were wrong, promptly admitted it.
11. Sought through prayer and meditation to improve our conscious contact with God as we understood Him, praying only for knowledge of His will for us and the power to carry that out.
12. Having made an effort to practice these principles in all our affairs, we tried to carry this message to other compulsive gamblers.

**The Twelve Steps of Overeaters Anonymous**

1. We admitted we were powerless over food—that our lives had become unmanageable.
2. Came to believe that a Power greater than ourselves could restore us to sanity.
3. Made a decision to turn our will and our lives over to the care of God *as we understood Him.*
4. Made a searching and fearless moral inventory of ourselves.
5. Admitted to God, to ourselves, and to another human being the exact nature of our wrongs.
6. Were entirely ready to have God remove all these defects of character.
7. Humbly asked Him to remove our shortcomings.
8. Made a list of all persons we had harmed, and became willing to make amends to them all.
9. Made direct amends to such people wherever possible, except when to do so would injure them or others.
10. Continued to take personal inventory and when we were wrong, promptly admitted it.
11. Sought through prayer and meditation to improve our conscious contact with God *as we understood Him,* praying only for knowledge of His will for us and the power to carry that out.
12. Having had a spiritual awakening as the result of these steps, we tried to carry this message to compulsive overeaters and to practice these principles in all our affairs.

## The Twelve Steps of Sex Addicts Anonymous

1. We admitted we were powerless over addictive sexual behavior—that our lives had become unmanageable.
2. Came to believe that a Power greater than ourselves could restore us to sanity.
3. Made a decision to turn our will and our lives over to the care of God as we understood God.
4. Made a searching and fearless moral inventory of ourselves.
5. Admitted to God, to ourselves, and to another human being the exact nature of our wrongs.
6. Were entirely ready to have God remove all these defects of character.
7. Humbly asked God to remove our shortcomings.
8. Made a list of all persons we had harmed and became willing to make amends to them all.
9. Made direct amends to such people wherever possible, except when to do so would injure them or others.
10. Continued to take personal inventory and when we were wrong promptly admitted it.
11. Sought through prayer and meditation to improve our conscious contact with God as we understood God, praying only for knowledge of God's will for us and the power to carry that out.
12. Having had a spiritual awakening as the result of these steps, we tried to carry this message to other sex addicts and to practice these principles in our lives.

**The Twelve Steps of Co-Dependents Anonymous**

1.  We admitted we were powerless over others—that our lives had become unmanageable.
2.  Came to believe that a power greater than ourselves could restore us to sanity.
3.  Made a decision to turn our will and lives over to the care of God as we understood God.
4.  Made a searching and fearless moral inventory of ourselves.
5.  Admitted to God, to ourselves, and to another human being, the exact nature of our wrongs.
6.  Were entirely ready to have God remove all these defects of character.
7.  Humbly asked God to remove our shortcomings.
8.  Made a list of all persons we had harmed and became willing to make amends to them all.
9.  Made direct amends to such people wherever possible, except when to do so would injure them or others.
10. Continued to take personal inventory and when we were wrong, promptly admitted it.
11. Sought through prayer and meditation to improve our conscious contact with God as we understood God, praying only for knowledge of God's will for us and the power to carry that out.
12. Having had a spiritual awakening as the result of these steps, we tried to carry this message to other co-dependents, and to practice these principles in all our affairs.

Adapted from the Twelve Steps of Alcoholics Anonymous with permission of AA World Services, Inc., New York, N.Y. (See author's note on copyright page.)

## The Twelve Steps of Emotions Anonymous

1. We admitted we were powerless over our emotions—that our lives had become unmanageable.
2. Came to believe that a Power greater than ourselves could restore us to sanity.
3. Made a decision to turn our will and our lives over to the care of God *as we understood Him.*
4. Made a searching and fearless moral inventory of ourselves.
5. Admitted to God, to ourselves and to another human being the exact nature of our wrongs.
6. Were entirely ready to have God remove all these defects of character.
7. Humbly asked Him to remove our shortcomings.
8. Made a list of all persons we had harmed, and became willing to make amends to them all.
9. Made direct amends to such people wherever possible, except when to do so would injure them or others.
10. Continued to take personal inventory and when we were wrong promptly admitted it.
11. Sought through prayer and meditation to improve our conscious contact with God *as we understood Him,* praying only for knowledge of His will for us and the power to carry that out.
12. Having had a spiritual awakening as the result of these steps, we tried to carry this message and to practice these principles in all our affairs.

# Appendix C
## Recommended Resources

Adult Children of Alcoholics
P.O. Box 3216
2522 West Sepulveda Boulevard, Suite 200
Torrance, CA 90510
310-534-1815

Al-Anon Family Headquarters, Inc./Alateen
1600 Corporate Landing Parkway
Virginia Beach, VA 23454-5617
888-4AL-ANON
http://www.al-anon.org

Alcoholics Anonymous General Service Office (AA)
475 Riverside Drive
New York, NY 10115
212-870-3400
http://www.alcoholics-anonymous.org

The American Academy of Medical Acupuncture
5820 Wilshire Boulevard, Suite 500
Los Angeles, CA 90036
323-937-5514

American Massage Therapy Association
820 Davis Street, Suite 100
Evanston, IL 60201-4444
847-864-0123

Center for Addiction and Alternative Medicine Research
914 South Eighth Street, Suite D-917
Minneapolis, MN 55404
612-347-7670

Christian Recovery International
P.O. Box 215
Brea, CA 92822

Cocaine Anonymous World Service Office (CA)
P.O. Box 2000
Los Angeles, CA 90049-8000
800-347-8998
http://www.ca.org

Co-Dependents Anonymous
P.O. Box 33577
Phoenix, AZ 85067-3577
602-277-7991
http://www.codependents.org

Emotions Anonymous International
P.O. Box 4245
St. Paul, MN 55104-0245
651-647-9712
http://www.emotionsanonymous.org

Gamblers Anonymous International Service Office
P.O. Box 17173
Los Angeles, CA 90017
213-386-8789
http://www.gamblersanonymous.org

JACS Foundation, Inc.
(Jewish Alcoholics, Chemically Dependent Persons and Significant Others)
426 West 58th Street
New York, NY 10019
212-397-4197
http://www.jacsweb.org/jacs
jacs@jacsweb.org

Narcotics Anonymous (NA)
World Services Office
P.O. Box 9999
Van Nuys, CA 91409
818-773-9999
http://www.na.org

National Acupuncture Detoxification Association
3220 N Street, NW #275
Washington, DC 20007
888-765-6232

National Association for Christian Recovery
P.O. Box 922
Yorba Linda, CA 92885

National Center for Homeopathy
801 North Fairfax Street, Suite 306
Alexandria, VA 22314
703-548-7790

Nicotine Anonymous World Services
P.O. Box 591777
San Francisco, CA 94159-1777
415-750-0328
http://www.nicotine-anonymous.org

Overeaters Anonymous World Service Office
6075 Zenith Ct. NE
Rio Rancho, NM 87124
505-891-2664
http://www.overeatersanonymous.org

Recoveries Anonymous Universal Services
P.O. Box 1212
East Northport, NY 11731
516-261-1212
http://www.r-a.org

Sex Addicts Anonymous
P.O. Box 70949
Houston, TX 77270
713-869-4902
http://www.sexaa.org
info@saa-recovery.org

Sexaholics Anonymous
P.O. Box 111910
Nashville, TN 37222
615-331-6230
http://www.sa.org

Sex and Love Addicts Anonymous
Fellowship-Wide Services, Inc.
P.O. Box 338
Newton, MA 02062-0338
781-255-8825
http://www.slaafws.org

Sexual Compulsives Anonymous
P.O. Box 1585
Old Chelsea Station, NY 10011
800-977-HEAL
http://www.sca-recovery.org

Sexual Recovery Anonymous
P.O. Box 73
New York, NY 10024
212-340-4650
http://ourworld.compuserve.com/homepages/sra

## Web Sites Worth Wandering

"Another Empty Bottle"
http://www.alcoholismhelp.com

12 Step Cyber Cafe
http://www.12steps.com

"Hope and Healing WebChronicles"
http://www.hopeandhealing.com

Information about Addictive Behavior
www.cts.com/crash/habtsmrt/

Links to Recovery
http://www.nb.net/~critter/recovery.htm

Marijuana Anonymous World Services
http://www.marijuana-anonymous.org

Sober Vacations
http://www.sobervacations.com/index.htm

Substance Abuse Issues
http://www.jointogether.org

If you are looking for more information on addiction and recovery issues, visit the world's largest recovery bookstore complete with books, videocassettes, audiocassettes, and chat rooms at www.hazelden.org/bookstore

## About the Author

Meredith Gould is a sociologist and writer whose work focuses on the practical, holistic aspects of relationships, recovery, and spiritual life. The author of *Tips for Your Home Office* (Storey, 1998), she lives in Princeton, New Jersey.

Hazelden Information and Educational Services is a division of the Hazelden Foundation, a not-for-profit organization. Since 1949, Hazelden has been a leader in promoting the dignity and treatment of people afflicted with the disease of chemical dependency. The mission of the foundation is to improve the quality of life for individuals, families, and communities by providing a national continuum of information, education, and recovery services that are widely accessible; to advance the field through research and training; and to improve our quality and effectiveness through continuous improvement and innovation.

Stemming from that, the mission of this division is to provide quality information and support to people wherever they may be in their personal journey—from education and early intervention, through treatment and recovery, to personal and spiritual growth.

Although our treatment programs do not necessarily use everything Hazelden publishes, our bibliotherapeutic materials support our mission and the Twelve Step philosophy upon which it is based. We encourage your comments and feedback.

The headquarters of the Hazelden Foundation is in Center City, Minnesota. Additional treatment facilities are located in Chicago, Illinois; New York, New York; Plymouth, Minnesota; St. Paul, Minnesota; and West Palm Beach, Florida. At these sites, we provide a continuum of care for men and women of all ages. Our Plymouth facility is designed specifically for youth and families.

For more information on Hazelden, please call **1-800-257-7800.** Or you may access our World Wide Web site on the Internet at **www.hazelden.org.**